Rural Visitors

A parish workbook for welcoming visitors in the country church

Rural Visitors

A parish workbook for welcoming visitors in the country church

Jeremy Martineau

and

Leslie J Francis

with illustrations by
Chris Bishop

First published in September 2001

Acora Publishing
Arthur Rank Centre
Stoneleigh Park
Warwickshire CV8 2LZ

All rights reserved. No part of this publication may be reproduced, stored in a retrieval system, or transmitted in any form, or by any means, electronic, mechanical, photocopying, recording, or otherwise, without the written permission of the publisher.

© Leslie J Francis and Jeremy Martineau, 2001
Cartoons by Chris Bishop
Cover Photo : Jeremy Martineau

The right of Leslie J Francis and Jeremy Martineau to be identified as the authors of this work has been asserted in accordance with the Copyright, Designs and Patents Act 1988.

ISBN 0 9540766 0 5

Typesetting by Acora Publishing,
Stoneleigh Park, Warwickshire CV8 2LZ

Printed by
NAC Print Services

Contents

	Page
Preface	vii
Introduction	1
Part One: First Principles	3
Part Two: Meeting the Visitors	13
Part Three: Listening to the Visitors	23
1 Someone to welcome you	24
2 News of church services	28
3 News of church events	32
4 News of local events	36
5 A guide book to buy	40
6 Simple free guide sheet	44
7 A book to write your name in	48
8 Somewhere to write prayer requests	52
9 Flowers	56
10 Music playing	60
11 Smell of incense	64
12 Candles to light	68
13 Suggestions for prayer	72
14 An open bible	76
15 Reserved sacrament	80
16 Somewhere quiet to pray	84
17 Christian book stall	88
18 Requests for donations	92
19 Access for the disabled	96
20 Gifts to buy	100
21 Information about other things to do in the area	104
22 Toilet	108
Appendix A - Useful books	113
Appendix B - Helpful organisations	114
Appendix C - Book shop suppliers	114
The survey form	115

Preface

This book is the fourth in a series which reflects the two authors' firm commitment to and clear confidence in the rural church. We are convinced that planning for the future of the rural church needs both to be grounded in high quality research and to be rooted in local reflection and initiative. *Rural Visitors* is a parish workbook which employs the findings of new research to help local churches reflect on their work among visitors and tourists both in the church and in the wider community. It is possible to conclude that many of the people who come to our rural churches as visitors and tourists are open to exploring something about the faith to which these churches were built to witness. This alone should encourage greater effort among churchgoers to engage with visitors and tourists.

We wish to record our gratitude to those who have assisted us in preparing this book. First, the organisation of the research supported by the National Churches Tourism Group has involved many clergy and lay people throughout the more rural parts of England and Wales. Without their help there could have been no book. Second, we record our gratitude to Chris Bishop for enlivening and enriching our words and figures with such entertaining and through-provoking illustrations. Finally, we record our gratitude to Mandy Robbins, Susan Thomas, Mike Fearn and Anna Halsall who helped shape the manuscript, and to Katrina Terrance who prepared the camera ready copy.

Leslie J Francis
University of Wales, Bangor

Jeremy Martineau
Arthur Rank Centre

August 2001

Introduction

Rural Visitors is a parish workbook designed to help rural churches reflect on their work among visitors and tourists both in the church and in the wider local community.

There are twenty-two sections to the third part of this workbook. Some churches may decide to use them all. Other churches may wish to select a few examples. Some churches may decide to explore several sections at one time. Other churches may wish to spend longer over a smaller number of sections.

Each section has been drafted in the same way. First, key statistics are presented from a recent survey conducted among more than twelve thousand people who have visited rural churches throughout England and Wales. Then these statistics are followed by questions for local study, and some suggested activities. These activities might well take place away from the normal place of worship, as well as within it. The authors also offer their own reflection on each of the twenty-two sections.

The survey from which these statistics was taken asked visitors and tourists to rural churches to rate on a five point scale how much they like to find certain features when they visit churches. The features ranged from 'somewhere quiet to pray' to 'information about other things to do in the area'.

Have you both come far?

Each set of statistics presents five pieces of key information. The opening statistics record the proportion of visitors and tourists who rate the feature four or five on the five point scale. Then the statistics distinguishing between the responses of the women and the men, between the responses of four different age groups, between the responses of those who live quite near-by and those who have travelled greater distances and between the responses of those who attend church most Sundays, those who attend church at least once a month, and those who attend church less often than monthly.

It is the writers' hope that discussion of these important issues will be conducted without pressure to make policy decisions. Such discussions can then inform and advise those who need to take such decisions.

Suggestions on using this workbook

To plan a discussion on topics such as these, ensure that participants have the relevant background information in advance. The group may work best with between eight and ten people. To cover such a wide range of viewpoints will require experienced group leadership skills; the function of the group leader is to facilitate discussion, not to impose his or her own views. By modelling listening the leader will enable others to listen. It is important to allow space and time for sharing personal experiences which give rise to present opinions.

The aim of a discussion on any of these topics is to increase knowledge and awareness of the interests and views of the people who visit rural churches. Sessions should not last more than ninety minutes. At the end of this time participants should be more aware of the origin and formation of their own views and those which others hold. They should have experienced difference as a positive contribution to life in the church.

It is often helpful for refreshments to be served on arrival. The leader or host should ensure that each person is known to everyone. To invite each person to say why they have come may be a useful way of opening the subject. It is more creative to use the time in different ways: working in twos or fours, by brainstorming ideas which are written on a flip chart, by using silence for a time of reflection, and only some time in plenary discussion. It is also important to recognise that extroverts feel much more at home with these group processes than introverts. It is important not to press introverts too hard into contributing in an extrovert way. Such pressure may just force them to stay away.

Part One

FIRST PRINCIPLES

First principles

Introduction

God is welcoming and inviting, as well as mysterious. God is already there, waiting for us to return. The places dedicated to God's service and worship should reflect these characteristics. Scripture tells us that Abraham's wife Sarah received angels, unaware, with courtesy, and with food as hospitality. In simple societies nothing is more important than making the visitor welcome.

Open the church

Over 40% of rural churches are kept unlocked during daytime (1995 research), thanks to the loving care and commitment of some faithful member(s). Many are unlocked all the time, perhaps because the key was lost decades ago. Many have a 'keyholder' notice which is a system so full of hazards that it is practically worthless. It gives the church the illusion of being open, but in practice few visitors make use of it. Keys can go missing; key holders worry about whether they should hand a key over to a stranger or whether they should go with the visitor to the church; key holders may themselves be vulnerable. This system works best in the case of a rarely visited church and where the key holder lives very close-by.

Locked churches give a clear message that God has gone away, and perhaps that the local church as a worshipping community has lost interest in making known the gospel of a welcoming God. Locking a church does little to defend the contents. Three times as many churches are broken into as are subject to damage or loss when unlocked. Locking is an understandable reaction in an area of repeated criminal damage. Damage caused by a forced entry can sometimes be more expensive to repair than the replacement of whatever has been stolen. Serious professional thieves cannot easily be deterred. They are just as likely to steal to order, wearing white coats and loading the lectern into a very visible van in front of the eyes of the congregation who may not comprehend what is happening.

Protective systems can include neighbourhood watch awareness schemes, automatic lights that are switched on by body movement, systems to protect moveable objects, and even closed circuit TV cameras. The dummy versions of CCTV can be very effective.

C.W? Oh no! not Church Warden, Church Watch.

Strongly recommended is the NACOSS approved remote signalling burglar and fire alarms (which send a signal to a 24hr monitoring centre). Discounts are available from the Ecclesiastical Insurance Group (www.eigonline.co.uk) off the insurance premium if either of these are fitted. There is also the National Churchwatch Scheme which is gathering momentum and is Home Office approved. Access to a local scheme is through the church's local police Crime Reduction Officer. The Website address is www.nationalchurchwatch.com

A good idea is to create secure areas within an open church, where valuables can be kept. Ideally this would be an area to which the public would not expect to have access. The vestry, for example, can be fitted with modern locks, alarms etc and the windows barred without affecting the atmosphere of the church. Safes are good, but old ones are surprisingly easy to break open from the back. Therefore any safe weighing less than a ton should be fixed to both wall and floor. Ecclesiastical Insurance Group surveyors will be very happy to offer free security advice to any of their insured churches.

In 1999 all churches insured by Ecclesiastical Insurance Group (92% of Anglican churches) were supplied with an 'Alphadot' microdot kit with which to mark their movable valuables. This system is well worth using as a church in Somerset found. An antique chair was identified in the possession of a man who said he had owned it for years. Without the Alphadots it would have been difficult to prove that this was not the stolen chair's twin.

The wish to open locked churches has lain behind the *Open Churches Trust*, founded by Andrew Lloyd Webber and the *Through the Church Door* project across the West Midlands. It is also one of the main objectives of the National Churches Tourism Group, now the leading focus for advising churches on how to minister to visitors.

Signpost the church

The locked door is not the first 'turn-off' encountered by well-meaning visitors. The absence of information and signposting can put off all but the most determined visitor. Whereas the sight of the tower or spire may suggest to the car-born visitor that there is a settlement which justifies a break in their journey, entering the villlage, among the trees the church is quite difficult to spot. The visitor is possibly not intent on visiting the church, although a visit may be made as part of a short stop for refreshments or just to see what kind of a place this is. The signpost that draws attention to the church should also indicate that it is open and visitors are welcome to call.

Making visitors welcome

Car parking near rural churches is frequently not clearly marked. To provide visitors with somewhere dry underfoot to 'dismount' is an indication of welcome. The entrance to many churchyards is guarded by a lychgate. Here may be the first place to convey the welcome in a positive way rather than by a notice making dire threats to those walking dogs. If you are serious about wanting visitors to come into the church then the access must be straightforward and clear. Since old churches may have several ancient doorways it is often difficult to know which door to try. In a world which increasingly does not understand that the church is for everyone, it may be necessary to invite people in and show them how to manage the challenge. Old wooden doors are designed for protection – an impression which will clearly deter many who are thus condemned to wander aimlessly with their thoughts in the burial ground. What a message with which to send your visitors away! Some churches provide self service tea and coffee facilities, and even a bowl of water in the porch for the dog.

Churchyards are visited by far more than those who dare to enter the church building itself. Churchyards may hold an important reservoir of fauna and flora, especially those managed under the Living Churchyard scheme. Contact the Arthur Rank Centre for full information on this. Churchyards certainly contain many epitaphs of historical interest or humour, as well as quiet belief in eternity. The opportunity to locate particular gravestones can take some visitors thousands of miles; links to associated graves can form a long trail of enquiry, tracing famous poets, artists, explorers or villains.

A moveable noticeboard saying 'Church Open: Welcome' is best, but can carry your own additional words, suggesting what the visitor can expect on entry, ranging from 'come in and pray' to 'mind the two steps down'.

First impressions

Now that we have managed to get the visitor's hand on the door handle, can we get them inside safely? An automatic light coming on as the door opens is both a safety feature if there are steps to negotiate, but also an effective deterrent to any unwelcome visitors who might have mischief in mind.

The layout of the church is normally for the benefit of the sedentary congregation. Seats, cupboards, everything is in place to meet the worshippers' needs. Most churches have far more seats occupying that lovely space than are normally required. Mediaeval churches were designed with open space naves; seats came later. Many are now trying to free up that space to carry information of interest to the visitor. Such information will range from dynamic displays of children's work used last week in the worship to expensively produced advertising about other visitor attractions in the area. It is possible to achieve a wide range of objectives in the way this space is used.

Demonstrate that this church is alive and well. Even the church rotas tell a story. The number of names on the list tell how many households are involved in the regular worship. Even small congregations can use photographs to indicate that it is real people that make up the active community of faith. Photographs of parish activities contribute to the positive message. Make sure all material is of the highest possible standard and fresh in appearance. Tatty material is counter-productive and tells the visitor that this is a tired church.

Local businesses which have an interest in visitors could be willing to sponsor a display which includes their business. Restaurants, accommodation, shops, arts and crafts, major visitor attractions all welcome visitors as customers. It may be to the church that visitors first come. In return other visitor oriented businesses will signpost visitors to the church. Churches are well advised to ensure that those other organisations and businesses with an interest in tourism in the locality have good quality and up to date information about the church, when it is open, its main items of interest as well as times of services. Such organisations as those that provide accommodation, the parish council with responsibility for the footpath map, British Waterways Board, caravan site managers and other attractions. Some churches provide information about where local food can be bought, including farm shops, farmers' markets, and restaurants that serve local produce. The Countryside Agency has such promotion as a priority in its 'Eat the View' campaign.

Many church visitors are relatively local and will benefit from seeing notices that show how well the church is a part of the whole life of your village. Parish councils will welcome the opportunity to have the parish footpath map displayed and available for visitors to use.

Encourage local people to bring their own family visitors to visit the church. This can increase their own appreciation and pride in the church and thus their 'ownership' of it.

Getting the Christian message across

Many visitors want to pray in the church, whether they are regular worshippers or not. Some may need modest help by providing words on prayer cards. Others respond to the possibility of prayer requests being prayed when the congregation meets for worship. Facilities to make this possible using post-its or a looseleaf book in the place identified as a place for prayer are effective. A growing number of people wish to 'light a candle' and prayer candle stands can now be found in churches of a wide range of traditions. Security against vandalism is important with combustible materials.

Even the hymn numbers from last week can be used to good effect. Leave them up. It is not untidy, but reminds visitors that worship happens here. Sacrifice a hymn book by cutting one up, enlarging one of last week's hymns and featuring it in an obvious place. As our theology is derived from hymns and scripture as much as from sermons, being able to read both hymns and passages from the bible will help people re-connect with perhaps long forgotten memories of faith. Similarly the bible on the lectern could be open at a key passage, changing each week, with a highlighted verse or two. Or sacrifice a bible in the same way as the hymn book. Use a spot light to focus on the key texts.

The main items of liturgical furniture offer an opportunity to explain to an increasingly ignorant generation about baptism as the water of life, cleansing and regenerating; lectern as the word of life and the strength of tradition and culture; altar as the rewards of self-giving and the place of sharing.

Few visitors find inspiration in the architectural niceties, and guide material is best written in simple language. A partnership between church and the local junior school can create a popular version for free take away guide leaflet, whereas the more traditional booklet with photographs for sale is more expensive to produce.

Explore ways in which the basics of the Christian faith can be expressed clearly and simply amidst the historical and architectural descriptions. It may be the chance of a lifetime.

What do visitors take away?

A signature in the visitors' book is a mark of appreciation. Visitors' books could helpfully have an extra column asking for information as to the size of the group on whose behalf the signer acts. Research suggests one in eight visitors sign the book. Loose-leaf books make the removal of unwelcome comments easy. Some visitors may be willing to receive regular reports from a favourite church, and become long distance supporters. The search for roots is an important part of the human journey. Our churches are, for many, way-markers or signposts, not a place to settle.

Most visitors expect to leave a donation. The average gift is only 20p (1999 figure) but with an opportunity to make a purchase this can be transformed. Cards with prayers or wise sayings are popular and can normally be safely left out in unstaffed churches. Picture postcards are relatively low income earners and move slowly. In our consumer society people welcome the chance to make a purchase, normally under £5.00. Even in unstaffed churches gift items can be displayed in a secure cabinet with information given about where they can be bought. Such a link with a local retail outlet, shop, garage or pub is of mutual benefit.

Churches that deliberately give something, such as a prayer card or bookmark, to departing visitors find that the level of donations rises significantly, well covering the cost of the gift.

Perhaps your community can provide a unique visitor experience based in the church building. Is your organist available to demonstrate the range of the instrument? Is a local artist willing to display work while showing his or her talent in an active way?

For churches which attract groups on a scheduled stop the opportunity to enrich the visitor experience are numerous, requiring little more than elementary administration. The financial rewards can be considerable. Be clear to coach operators, coach drivers and group secretaries about what they can expect and whether this may include a short guided tour, refreshments, a demonstration of music, art or craft. Such commercial tours should expect to pay between 50p

- £1 per visitor for the added value you provide, in addition to any voluntary personal contributions.

Who is going to do all this?

The good news is that local people are proud of their church building, even if they use it infrequently. Among the whole community there will be a small number who might be willing to be drawn into the demanding but rewarding task of helping the building relate more effectively to visitors. A task force made up of lay people should be given the job of devising an action plan involving all the matters outlined above. At least one member of the church council should be on this task force. The force leader should be a member of the church council. Churches in the wider area will be able to achieve much more by cooperation than by competition. The National Churches Tourism Group is keen to help by running seminars for churches across a wide area. Such events have often been an occasion for discovering rich resources of skill and professionalism among lay people to the benefit of churches across a wider area.

Every local authority has a tourism officer, normally within the economic development department. Quite frequently these officers are keen to hear that churches wish to take ministry to visitors seriously. These officers can bring expertise and maybe access to modest funds to help with the necessary work of providing for visitor needs and especially with marketing. The tourism officer is a vital ally, and their advice and help should be sought at the outset.

12 Rural Visitors

There is an understandable interest in creating church trails, a simple cooperative marketing tool. However most visitors to churches are making casual rather than planned visits to churches and an appropriate marketing strategy could be in conjunction with dissimilar local businesses. To help visitors spend longer in one place is a core strategy of sustainable tourism, for it contributes more to the local economy.

In recent years other specialist organisations have recognised their own potential in tourism. The British Horse Society has created greenways, using bridle paths, to attract more horseriders and equestrian businesses. Many of the old ways of moving about the country, open to riders and walkers, not surprisingly connect churches, especially those 'off the beaten track'. Sustrans' great project to open up long distance safe-from-cars cycle routes is opening up other older routes. British Waterways have an obvious network of canals and navigable rivers, which provide other connections to old settlements with their churches. Church tourism work needs to recognise the variety of ways in which visitors might find their way into the area, when planning a marketing strategy. The local authority tourism officer can be a great help in understanding this larger picture.

What about charging?

Many people feel affronted by being asked to pay to enter a house of prayer. The most satisfactory solution for churches other than cathedrals is to identify special places to which entry can be controlled, such as a tower or crypt, access to which is by payment. Health and safety issues abound in these conditions and advice should be sought, but the rewards can be significant. One rural church earns £10,000 a year from those who climb the tower. An emergency rescue plan should be prepared - see Appendix A.

Part Two

MEETING THE VISITORS

Meeting the visitors

Introduction

In order to learn more about the people who visit rural churches a number of churches were invited to participate in a nation-wide survey. A total of 165 churches accepted the invitation and displayed a prominent notice asking visitors to complete the simple and attractive questionnaire. The completed questionnaires were collected in a clearly marked post-box in the church.

The 12,679 questionnaires completed by the church visitors provide an unique source of information about who is currently visiting our churches in rural England and in rural Wales. This section looks in turn at what can be learnt from discussing the ratio between male and female visitors, their age profile, their pattern of church attendance, whether they are visiting alone or as part of a group, their mode of transport, the distance they have travelled, and how many churches they have visited in recent days.

Sex

male	36%
female	64%

The fact that twice as many women visit our churches compared with men is fascinating for two reasons. The first point is that these figures match very closely the ratio between men and women who attend church services. This suggests from the outset that the appeal of church tourism may have something in common with the wider appeal of religion itself. This suggestion is worth closer scrutiny.

While there is no dispute about the empirical fact that women are more likely to attend church services than men and that women tend to be more religious overall than men, there is considerable dispute about the theories advanced to account for this difference between the sexes. Classically sociologists of religion have argued that women's place in society gives them more time for religion and a greater need for the comfort and support that religion provides. While significant social changes in the past few decades have eroded the apparent power of this explanation, the empirical fact has remained that women are still more religious than men.

Psychologists of religion, on the other hand, have argued that religion appeals to a particular kind of personality which may be more often found among women, but is there among men as well. Psychologists talk about the gender dimensions of femininity and masculinity which are present in varying degrees among both men and women. On this account religion appeals to the *gender* difference of femininity rather than to the *sex* difference of being female.

The second point is that, if church tourism appeals to the femininity personality profile of men and women, churches can be shaped to speak to the wider dimensions of this personality preference. The psychological appeal of femininity embraces a wide range of the aesthetic arts, including those which speak to the senses of sight, sound, smell, touch, and taste. Here is the psychological rationale for enriching our country churches with music, incense, pictures, and textures.

Age

under 12 years	5%
12-19 years	11%
20-39 years	16%
40-59 years	37%
over 60 years	31%

The fact that over two thirds of those who visit our churches are in the second half of life also matches the age profile of church congregations. Four key points emerge from a clear recognition of the age profile of our church tourists. It is perhaps sensible to discuss these points beginning from the oldest group.

First, 31% of church visitors are aged sixty or over. This group includes some who are still in employment, the active early retired and the less active aging retired population. Retirement may bring more available time for tourism, but this may be restricted by less disposable income. Aging may be accompanied by restrictions on mobility, sight and hearing. In other words, local churches need to be sensitive to the particular needs of aging visitors in terms of safe access, good lighting and large print materials.

I bet the next person to come through that door will be a middle aged woman who may be hard of hearing and has lost touch with her roots...well, that's what those reseachers said.

Second, 37% of church visitors are in their forties or fifties. This is a group of people who may have lost touch with their own church roots during their teenage years, their twenties and their thirties. For some this is a period when children may be leaving home and when there is both time and need to rethink priorities in life. Meaningful contact with the church through tourism could be of crucial significance to the age group.

Third, 16% of church visitors are in their twenties and thirties. This is an age group largely absent from church congregations. For this reason contact with this age group through church tourism could be of major significance in reminding young adults and young parents of the values and beliefs proclaimed by the church. This is an age group which may carry specific concerns and anxieties over relationships, family life, parenting and employment. Such issues could be readily addressed by the literature available in the local church.

Fourth, 16% of church visitors are children and young people under the age of twenty. Here are young people who may still be curious about church buildings and the messages which these buildings convey. Those churches which produce literature and trails for the young may be making excellent use of their resources.

Church attendance

once a week	41%
once a month	15%
once a year	14%
less often	30%

These statistics make it clear that there are two kinds of church tourists. The expectations and needs of these two groups might be quite different.

On the one hand, 41% of those who visit rural churches are themselves weekly churchgoers. These individuals are likely to be interested in and well informed about a variety of aspects of church life and practice. The fact that many of these churchgoers are away from home and possibly on holiday may offer them time to reflect on their faith and to develop their commitment. It is important that local churches provide appropriate resources to people of this nature.

On the other hand, 30% of those who visit rural churches are people who have very little other contact with the church. They attend services less than once a year and stand largely outside church life. The fact that many of these non-churchgoers are away from home and possibly on holiday may offer them unique opportunities to reflect on their lifestyle and to reconsider their priorities and commitments. It is important that local churches provide appropriate resources for people of this nature as well.

The remaining 29% of those who visit rural churches have a more casual relation with the church. They are not weekly churchgoers, but they are people who attend church from time to time. Being away from home and having time to visit rural churches may speak to such individuals in a way different from that experienced by weekly churchgoers and by non-churchgoers.

Social visiting

visiting alone	9%
visiting with one other person	44%
visiting with two or three others	30%
visiting with four or more others	17%

For the majority of tourists church visiting is a social rather than a solitary activity. Only 9% of visitors are visiting alone. There are enormous implications from this fact for the way in which churches prepare to welcome visitors.

The solitary visitor may wish to slip into the church unobserved, to find a quiet corner, to pray in solitude, to light a candle and to pour in peace over a passage of scripture in order to hear the word of God and to listen to God's prompting. The very last thing which some solitary visitors wish to find is a custodian to greet them, to talk with them and to observe them.

The social visitor may yearn for the very same experiences and yet feel unable to access the privacy crucial to such experiences. Religion has become an intensely personal and private matter. In our culture people are easily embarrassed being seen to be religious in public.

Many secular tourist attractions have now learnt how to generate private space in a social or public context and they do so through audio visual presentations. While individuals may feel uncomfortable sitting by themselves reading silently a passage from scripture, a group of people will huddle round the television screen listening to a video recording of the gospel read at the midnight Christmas service, or listening to the local vicar explaining the significance of the baptism service. Social visitors may be reluctant to kneel to say the Lord's prayer by themselves, but will pause revently while a brief prayer is conducted in the church. Living churches are places where social visitors experience the faith being lived out.

One in twenty (5%) of the visitors arrived in parties of 20 or more. Such visitors clearly belong to a more organised form of tourism. Cooperation between local churches and tour operators could open up all sorts of communication with visitors. Here is a very good opportunity not only to conduct tourists around the architecture, but also to show how the church is the centre of a living faith.

Modes of transport

car	74%
foot	16%
public transport	8%
bicycle	2%

The majority of church tourism (74%) is undertaken as part of the motor car culture. These tend to be people who are away from home seeking appropriate and enjoyable recreational activity. Some may be visiting a church because they are particularly interested in churches, but many may be doing so simply because the church happens to be there. To attract casual tourists of this nature, local churches need to ensure that the church is well sign-posted, that there is convenient parking, that access is straightforward between the car park and the church, and that tourists are made to feel welcome to visit.

OPEN AIR CHURCH
COME IN
PLUG IN
To
THE REV'D LYN

Casual tourists may need to be enticed into engaging with the local church. They may not come already knowing what to look for or what to expect. Some secular tourist attractions deal with this situation well by providing a pre-recorded message and headphones in the entrance area. This may be taken more seriously than printed material.

Casual tourists visiting by car may be attracted to find that the church they have chosen to visit is part of a group of churches linked by a rural trail. A printed map and directions may encourage some tourists to visit several of the neighbouring churches. As part of a tourist trail a network of churches could each emphasise a different aspect of the gospel message.

Casual tourists may also benefit from knowing about local shops, garages, eating places, and bed and breakfast accommodation. Indeed a consortium of local businesses might benefit from sponsoring the local rural church trail.

Distance from home

under 10 miles   11%
10-30 miles   15%
over 30 miles   62%
outside UK   12%

Three main points emerge from an analysis of the distance travelled by those who visit our rural churches.

First, this analysis confirms that the majority of visitors (74%) are at least 30 miles away from home and many of them are much further away than that. Knowledge of the local area cannot, therefore, be assumed among many of the visitors. This fact should influence the kind of information which local churches consider it appropriate to provide. For example, tourists away from home may need to know about local chemists and doctors. They might like to know that local church leaders are available to talk with them. They might like to find bed and breakfast at the vicarage or with the churchwarden. They might need more detailed information to locate the local keyholder (if the church is generally kept locked).

Second, this analysis makes it clear that between one in every eight and one in every nine visitors has come from overseas. Local churches may wish to look carefully at their visitors' book to see if there are particular countries from which their overseas visitors tend to come. Such information should help to shape the way in which specific interests of visitors are addressed. For example, if there is a steady flow of visitors from Spain it may be helpful to provide a brief leaflet in Spanish and to identify any local church members who welcome the opportunity to practice their Spanish.

Third, although nearly three quarters of the visitors travel from a distance, it is important to recognise that one in ten (11%) belongs to a local radius of ten miles. Although they do not live within the parish, such people might be interested in returning to that church for special events. In this context a long term calendar might be helpful, noting summer concerts, Christmas carol services and specialist interests addressed by the local church, like Taize services, liturgical dance, plainsong compline, New Testament Greek classes, and so on.

Number of churches visited

one	49%
two	21%
three	12%
four or more	18%

In the survey tourists were asked how many churches they had visited in the past seven days other than for worship. Their answers reveal two main points.

First, for half of the visitors (49%) the church at which they had completed the questionnaire was the only church visited in the seven day period. These, therefore, are not people who are making a point of travelling round from church to church. Their visiting is specific and special. In other words, opportunities lost by the church they have chosen to visit will not be compensated for by other churches earlier or later in the week. If the visit is specific and special for the visitor, it needs also to be seen as specific and special for the local church.

Second, for nearly a third of the visitors (30%) church tourism is a more significant part of their leisure activities, having visited at least three churches in a seven day period. Not only may the expectations and needs of the more professional church tourists differ from those of the tourists who visit just one church, but such individuals may themselves be developing a body of expertise which they could share with the local churches they visit.

22 Rural Visitors

Part Three

LISTENING TO THE VISITORS

Reading the statistics

The percentages in the following tables all refer to the proportion of visitors who rate the feature four or five on the five point scale.

The first percentage on each page gives the *overall* proportion of visitors. For example, in section one, 36% of the visitors rate having 'someone to welcome' them four or five on the five point scale.

The subsequent percentages distinguish between the responses of the women and the men, between the responses of four different age groups, between the responses of those who live quite near-by and those who have travelled greater distances, and between the responses of those who attend church most Sundays, those who attend church at least once a month, and those who attend church less often than monthly.

1 Someone to welcome you

Overall   36%

Sex

male	34%
female	36%

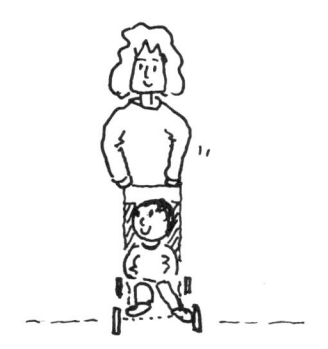

Age

12-19	46%
20-39	27%
40-59	29%
60 and over	42%

Distance travelled

under 10 miles	44%
10 miles plus	35%
outside UK	33%

Church attendance

weekly	43%
monthly	38%
less often	27%

Listening to the statistics

- Finding someone there to welcome them is important to one in every three (36%) of the people who visit rural churches. It is not so important to the other two in every three visitors (64%).

- There is no significant difference in the proportions of men and women (34% and 36%) who feel that it is important to find someone to welcome them when they visit rural churches.

- There are important differences in the expectations of different age groups on this matter. The youngest age group (12-19 year olds) and the eldest age group (those aged 60 and over) both attach more importance to finding someone to welcome them than is the case among the two middle age groups (20-59 years).

- Those who live less than 10 miles from the church are more likely to appreciate someone in the church to welcome them than is the case among those who have travelled greater distance.

- There is a very clear link between the visitors' own pattern of church attendance and their views on finding someone in the church to welcome them. While 43% of those who attend church services weekly like to find someone to welcome them, the proportion falls to 27% among those who attend church services less than once a month.

Rural Visitors

Activity

Use role play to explore the interaction between the person on welcoming duty in the local church and two visitors. One visitor is a weekly churchgoer from a nearby parish, while the other visitor is someone who never attends church and has travelled from the other side of the country.

Talking points

- Why do you feel that some people like to find someone to welcome them when they visit a rural church?

- Why do you feel that some people actually dislike finding someone to welcome them when they visit a rural church?

- Why do you feel that 12-19 year olds are more likely than 20-59 year olds to appreciate someone being there to welcome them when they visit a rural church?

- Why do you feel that people over the age of 60 are more likely than 20-59 year olds to appreciate someone being there to welcome them when they visit a rural church?

- Why are local people who live within a ten mile radius more likely than those who have travelled further distances to like someone to be there to welcome them?

- Why are people who do not attend church regularly less likely than those who attend every week to appreciate finding someone to welcome them when they visit rural churches?

Reflection

Some rural churches provide a rota of lay chaplains or custodians to be in the building at certain times. There can be three very positive benefits from such schemes.

First, there is a benefit for the security of the building itself. The building is less vulnerable to vandalism, damage and theft if it is known that custodians are there regularly. At the same time, it is important to ensure appropriate security for the custodians themselves.

Second, there is a benefit for some of the visitors. Some people may visit a church seeking forms of comfort, support, advice, or information. It is important therefore, that lay chaplains are properly trained to know how to deal with the range of issues which may come their way. They need to know which issues to refer to others and how to do so. At the same time, it is important to remember that some people who visit rural churches do so seeking privacy and quiet.

Third, there is a benefit for some of the lay chaplains or custodians themselves. Spending time in the local church to welcome visitors can develop as a very effective personal ministry. It can also provide the space and context in which to develop personal spirituality, reflection, and prayer.

2 News of church services

Overall 41%

Sex

| male | 38% |
| female | 43% |

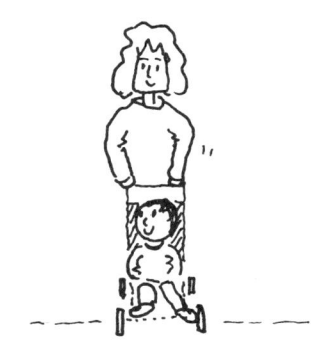

Age

12-19	42%
20-39	37%
40-59	40%
60 and over	46%

Distance travelled

under 10 miles	50%
10 miles plus	41%
outside UK	32%

Church attendance

weekly	57%
monthly	42%
less often	24%

Listening to the statistics

- Finding news of church services is important to two in every five (41%) of the people who visit rural churches. It is not so important to the other three in every five visitors (59%).

- Women who visit rural churches are just slightly more likely than men to want to find news of church services (43% compared with 38%).

- There are some interesting differences in the proportions of the various age groups who wish to find news of church services. The age group least likely to be interested in finding news of church services comprises the 20-39 year olds (37%). The age group most likely to be interested in finding news of church services comprises those aged 60 and over (46%).

- Those who live less than 10 miles from the church are more likely to appreciate news of church services than is the case among those who have travelled greater distances.

- There is a very clear link between the visitors' own pattern of church attendance and their views on finding news of church services. While 57% of those who attend church services weekly like to find news of church services, the proportion falls to 24% among those who attend church services less than once a month.

Activity

Examine the information which is displayed about church services at your church. How easy is it for visitors to find out what services are taking place? Explore the advantages and disadvantages of new ways of making known information about your services.

Talking points

- Why should as many as 41% of the visitors to rural churches be interested in news of church services?

- Why is a slightly higher proportion of women than men interested in news of church services?

- How do you explain the higher level of interest in news of church services among those aged 60 and over?

- How do you explain the higher level of interest in news of church services among those who live within a ten mile radius of the church which they are visiting?

- What do you make of the fact that one in four of the visitors who do not attend church regularly themselves are nonetheless interested in news of church services?

Reflection

Some rural churches give the impression that the only people who want or need to know about church services are the regular members who come to services most weeks. Several surveys of rural churches have drawn attention to the way in which some churches provide no information about services at all, while other churches display out-of-date information. The problem with out-of-date information is that people may turn up for services which are advertised but do not actually take place.

Services

11 o'clock Matins To celebrate the defeat of the Armada.

Followed by Mead and Biscuits

There are two very good reasons for rural churches to provide news of church services. First, the pattern of services in rural churches has changed dramatically in recent years. When services happen at different times on different Sundays, or happen only on certain Sundays, even local people may need accessible information about them. There may also be a growing tendency for occasional worshippers living in the countryside to try to find out about convenient service times in several local churches on those Sundays when they wish to attend.

Second, rural churches need to be seen not as unused museums but as the home of living Christian communities. Services are key occasions when those living Christian communities meet and worship. Offering visitors news of services can be so much more than simply posting the service times for the following week. A display screen can be used to show photographs of major services, like the harvest festival. Audio tapes can be used to provide a three minute highlight from the patronal festival. A short video can be used to show the Sunday morning communion service. News of how the church worships may encourage others to come to participate.

3 News of church events

Overall 40%

Sex

male	36%
female	43%

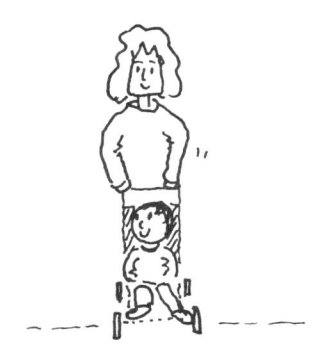

Age

12-19	47%
20-39	34%
40-59	37%
60 and over	42%

Distance travelled

under 10 miles	49%
10 miles plus	40%
outside UK	31%

Church attendance

weekly	51%
monthly	42%
less often	28%

Listening to the statistics

- Finding news of church events is important to two in every five (40%) of the people who visit rural churches. It is not so important to the other three in every five visitors (60%).

- Women who visit rural churches are slightly more likely than men to want to find news of church events (43% compared with 36%).

- There are some interesting differences in proportions of the various age groups who wish to find news of church events. The age group least likely to be interested in finding news of church events comprises the 20-39 year olds (34%). The age group most likely to be interested in finding news of church events comprises the 12-19 year olds (47%).

- Those who live less than 10 miles from the church are more likely to appreciate news of church events than is the case among those who have travelled greater distances.

- There is a very clear link between the visitor's own pattern of church attendance and their views on finding news of church events. While 51% of those who attend church services weekly like to find news of church events, the proportion falls to 28% among those who attend church services less than once a month.

Activity

Brainstorm a list of all the events which are associated with the local church. Include the major annual events like the Harvest Supper, the Christmas Bazaar, the Summer Fête. Include the regular events like the PCC meeting, bell-ringing practice, prayer groups, and children's groups. Discuss how these events and activities could be made known in the church and in the wider community. Should the local media be informed on a regular basis about what is happening in the church?

Talking points

- How can we respond to the fact that two out of every five visitors to rural churches would like to know about church events?

- What kind of news about church events is most likely to appeal to men and to women?

- What kind of news about church events is most likely to appeal to 12-19 year olds?

- In light of the high level of interest in news of church events among those who live within a ten mile radius of the church which they are visiting, how can your church respond to this interest?

- What do you make of the fact that more than one in four of the visitors who do not attend church regularly themselves are nonetheless interested in news of church events?

Reflection

So many rural churches may seem to their visitors to be little more than empty shells. To those in the know, however, these apparently empty shells provide the home for a vibrant and active community. The fact that the rural church is alive and well is one of the best kept secrets of the countryside.

A careful look beneath the surface, however, quickly begins to identify just how much is really going on in the life of so many of these churches. With a little care and planning so much more can be made of the major annual events, like the Harvest Supper, the Christmas Bazaar, or the Summer Fête. So much more can be made of the regular activities like bell-ringing practice and children's clubs.

*It's really caught on,
especially with our church being so close to the continent.*

A photographic record of the annual events and the regular activities can be displayed in the church. Such displays serve two purposes. They can enrich the experience of visitors by adding to the interest provided within the church. They can help to show visitors that the rural church is a vibrant and attractive community.

It is important to remember that displays and photographs tend to deteriorate quite quickly in conditions which may be cold and damp. Churches which are serious about profiling their activities and events in this way need to update their displays regularly. This responsibility could become an important ministry for a keen and competent photographer within the church.

4 News of local events

Overall   40%

Sex

male	36%
female	42%

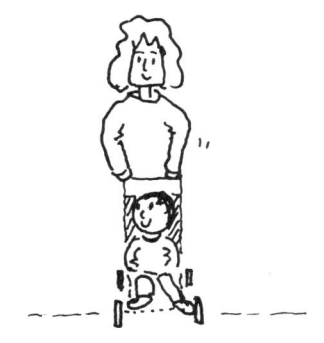

Age

12-19	50%
20-39	39%
40-59	36%
60 and over	35%

Distance travelled

under 10 miles	51%
10 miles plus	39%
outside UK	32%

Church attendance

weekly	39%
monthly	44%
less often	38%

Listening to the statistics

- Visitors to rural churches show the same overall level of interest in news about local events as they show in news of church events. Two in five (40%) show an interest in both areas.

- Women who visit rural churches are more likely than men to show an interest in news of church events and in news of local events, although the differences between the sexes is not that large.

- Visitors under the age of forty are likely to show slightly more interest in news of local events than in news of church events. Visitors aged sixty and over are likely to show slightly less interest in news of local events than in news of church events.

- Those who live less than ten miles from the church are more likely to appreciate news of local events than is the case among those who have travelled greater distances.

- While interest in news of church events is very clearly correlated with the visitor's own pattern of church attendance, this is not the case with interest in news of local events. Almost the same proportions of weekly churchgoers (39%) and of those who attend church less than monthly (38%) indicate an interest in discussing news of local events when they visit rural churches.

Activity

Brainstorm a list of all the local events which are not specifically church events. Begin with those in the local community, including events like outings for the retired, the bowls club, the darts team in the local pub, the luncheon club, delivery of meals-on-wheels, pre-school facilities, the Parish Council. Then consider events in the wider area which impact on the local community. Explore the extent to which church members are involved in these events and activities. Discuss which of these events and activities could be made known to the church.

Talking points

- Why are visitors to rural churches just as interested in news of local events as they are in news of church events?

- What kind of news about local events is most likely to appeal to men and women?

- What kind of news about local events is most likely to appeal to those aged 60 and over?

- How can the local community best respond to the fact that half of those visitors who live within a ten mile radius show an interest in finding out about local events when they visit the church.

- What do you make of the fact that those visitors also are not themselves regular churchgoers are more interested in learning about local events than they are in learning about church events.

Reflection

In many rural communities there remain clear links between the parish church and wider community life. This is the case for two reasons.

First, many of the individuals who are at the heart of community activities are also frequent or occasional worshippers at the local church. For example, there is usually some overlap between membership of the Parish Council and of the Parochial Church Council. Often church members are well motivated to become involved in aspects of pastoral care within the local community, like luncheon clubs for the elderly.

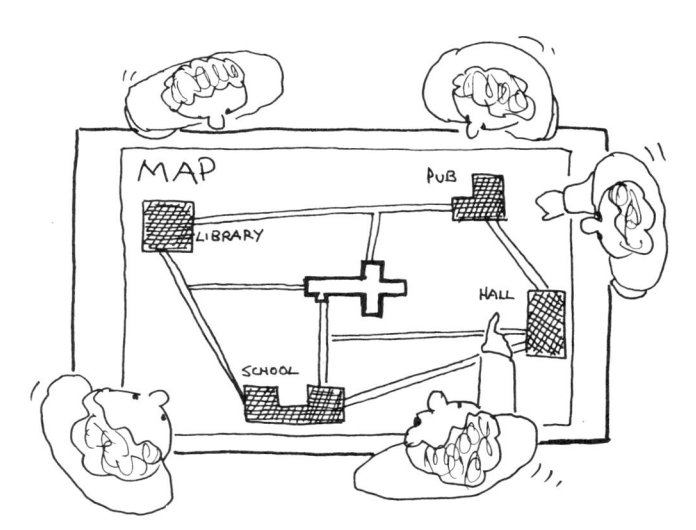

The New Village of St Matthew's, Plebley, Slopshire

Second, because of the very physical prominence of the church building within the local community, the church often remains a reference point for other secular local activities.

Using display screens in the church to profile local activities and events may achieve a lot more than simply enriching the experiences of church visitors. It may also help to strengthen the link between the church and the local community. There may be local people in the community who are not closely involved in the life of the church who would be interested in profiling local events and activities within the parish church.

From the outset, however, if space is to be provided in the parish church for profiling local events and activities, it is important to establish the lines of accountability for what is displayed and how displays are later dismantled and the materials dispersed.

5 A guide book to buy

Overall 54%

Sex

	male	54%
	female	54%

Age

	12-19	53%
	20-39	48%
	40-59	53%
	60 and over	60%

Distance travelled

	under 10 miles	59%
	10 miles plus	54%
	outside UK	44%

Church attendance

	weekly	54%
	monthly	57%
	less often	52%

Listening to the statistics

- Over half (54%) of the people who visit rural churches would like to find a guide book to buy.

- Men and women visitors to rural churches show an equal level of interest in finding a guide book to buy.

- The age group most attracted to buying guide books comprises those aged sixty and over (60%). The age group least attracted to buying guide books comprises those in their twenties and thirties (48%).

- Those who live less than 10 miles from the church are the most likely to express an interest in finding a guide book to buy. Visitors from outside the UK are the least likely to express an interest in finding a guide book to buy.

- There is no clear correlation between the visitors' own pattern of church attendance and their views on finding a guide book to buy. Thus, 54% of those who attend church services weekly express interest in finding a guide book to buy, and so do 52% of those who attend church services less than once a month.

Activity

Arrange a collection of guide books produced by different churches. Compare these with the guide books available in your church. Brainstorm the information which you would like to find in guide books, when you visit churches. Is a new guide book needed in your church, and, if so, how could this be produced?

Talking points

- Why do so many visitors to rural churches express an interest in finding a guide book to buy?

- Why are older church visitors (aged 60 and over) more likely than younger visitors to express an interest in finding a guide book to buy?

- Why are local people who live within a ten mile radius more likely than those who have travelled further distances to express an interest in finding a guide book to buy?

- What do you make of the fact that visitors who attend church services less often than once a month are just as interested in finding a guide book to buy as is the case among visitors who attend church services every week?

Reflection

Guide books available for sale in rural churches can serve at least three purposes.

First, guide books can enhance the visitor's experience by providing accessible information about the church. To achieve this purpose the text needs to be clearly set out with short descriptions which can be read while the visitor is looking round the church.

Second, guide books can provide a souvenir to be taken home to remind the purchaser of their visit. To achieve this purpose the book needs to be attractively produced and stored in conditions which keep the copies clean and smart.

Third, guide books can provide some interpretation which helps the building to say something about the contemporary Christian community and about the gospel which informs that community. To achieve this purpose care and sensitivity needs to be taken in linking this information to the visual attractions of the church.

Investment in the production and design of guide books can be seen as a good contribution to the wider mission of the church through the ability of guide books to communicate with a wider range of visitors, including both young and old, and including both regular churchgoers and those who have little other contact with the church.

6 Simple free guide sheet

Overall 72%

Sex

male	68%
female	75%

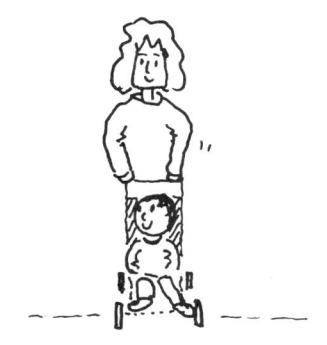

Age

12-19	72%
20-39	69%
40-59	72%
60 and over	75%

Distance travelled

under 10 miles	73%
10 miles plus	72%
outside UK	73%

Church attendance

weekly	74%
monthly	72%
less often	70%

Listening to the statistics

- Nearly three quarters (72%) of the people who visit rural churches would like to find a simple free guide sheet.

- Women who visit rural churches are more likely than men to want to find a simple free guide sheet (75% compared with 68%).

- The age group most interested in finding a simple free guide sheet comprises those aged sixty and over (75%). The age group least interested in finding a simple free guide sheet comprises those in their twenties and thirties (69%).

- The distance travelled to reach the church has no impact on the visitors' likely interest in finding a simple free guide sheet.

- Visitors to rural churches who are not themselves regular churchgoers are almost as likely as visitors who attend services each week to like to find a simple free guide sheet (70% compared with 74%).

Activity

If the church has a simple free guide sheet, take a fresh look at this publication and assess whether it is in need of revision or of modernising. If the church does not possess a simple free guide sheet, brainstorm the key information which could be included and how it could be designed.

Talking points

- Why do so many visitors to rural churches express an interest in finding a simple free guide sheet?

- What information do you think visitors want to find on a simple free guide sheet?

- How much information do you think people are willing to read on a simple free guide sheet?

- People who live within a ten mile radius of the church they are visiting are much more likely than visitors who have travelled greater distances to express an interest in *buying* a guide book. However distance makes no difference to interest in finding a simple free guide sheet. What do you see as the significance of this information?

- Would churchgoers and non-churchgoers expect to find the same kind of material in a simple free guide sheet?

Reflection

Simple free guide sheets can be quite cheap to print or to photocopy. They can enhance the visitors' experience while visiting the church and also provide a useful reminder of the visit in days to come.

Two main points are worth keeping in mind when designing such guide sheets. First, visitors are often looking for something which is quite short and easy to read. One effective way of achieving this is by providing a plan of the church, numbering the points of interest, and providing a one line comment on each numbered point.

It says this window was built in 1490, and isn't it good of them to lay on a ladder for visitors?

Second, visitors often value more highly something which is professionally produced and printed on good quality paper. Perhaps the cost of doing this can be offset by a local business (shop, garage, builder, undertaker) sponsoring the production in return for a credit line.

A simple free guide sheet could also note the times of church services, print a short prayer, or offer a passage from scripture. All of these help to create a link between the building which the visitor came to see and the on-going life and witness of the Christian community.

7 A book to write your name in

Overall 51%

Sex

male	46%
female	53%

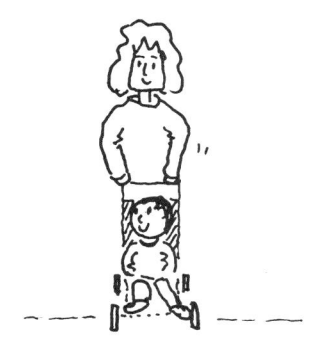

Age

12-19	70%
20-39	48%
40-59	42%
60 and over	47%

Distance travelled

under 10 miles	56%
10 miles plus	50%
outside UK	49%

Church attendance

weekly	47%
monthly	55%
less often	51%

Listening to the statistics

- About half (51%) of the people who visit rural churches would like to find a visitors' book in which to write their name.

- Women who visit rural churches are somewhat more inclined than men visitors to like to find a visitors' book in which to write their name (53% compared with 46%).

- It is the young visitors between the ages of 12 and 19 years who show the most interest in finding a book in which to write their names (70%). It is the visitors in their forties and fifties who show the least interest in signing visitors' books (42%).

- Visitors who live within a ten mile radius of the church they are visiting are more likely to show an interest in visitors' books, compared with visitors who have travelled further distances.

- Visitors who do not attend their own church on a weekly basis are more likely than weekly churchgoers to show an interest in signing visitors' books.

Well I never, Dear! Elvis was here last week!

Activities

Look at the visitors' book in your church. Consider how many visitors sign the book, where they come from, and the kind of comments they write in. Discuss whether the visitors' book could be improved by redesigning the page, for example providing more or less space for comment. Review whether the visitors' book is placed in the best location in the church and whether enough pens are available for visitors.

Talking points

- Why do half of the people who visit rural churches consider it important to find a book in which to write their name?

- Why are women who visit rural churches more interested than men visitors in finding a book in which to write their name?

- Why should young people under the age of twenty be so much more interested than older people in signing visitors' books when they visit rural churches?

- Why are people who live within a ten mile radius of the church they are visiting more likely to want to find a book in which to write their name?

- Why are weekly churchgoers less likely than people who attend church less frequently to be interested in finding a visitors' book in the churches they visit?

Reflection

The fascination with signing a visitors' book seems to be quite deep seated. There are two advantages in churches taking this fascination seriously.

For the visitors, signing the visitors' book provides them with the opportunity to record their visit and to see that they have woven their own identity into the rich and developing tapestry of the churches they visit. For some visitors this may add a sense of active participation to their experience.

For the churches, signatures in the visitors' book provides them with a record of the people who have visited. For some churches this may contribute to their sense of serving and ministering to tourists.

Care taken over the design of visitors' books can be a good investment for the local church. Given enough space and a good design visitors books could help to provide a profile of who is visiting specific churches. Opportunities can also be given for visitors making comments about their experience.

Some churches have written to those who have signed the visitors' book, say at Christmas time. For some this is a gesture of outreach and goodwill. For others it is part of a fund raising strategy.

8 Somewhere to write prayer requests

Overall   42%

Sex

male	36%
female	45%

Age

12-19	52%
20-39	42%
40-59	38%
60 and over	37%

Distance travelled

under 10 miles	48%
10 miles plus	42%
outside UK	35%

Church attendance

weekly	50%
monthly	45%
less often	32%

Listening to the statistics

- Two out of every five (42%) visitors to rural churches would welcome somewhere to write prayer requests.

- Women are more likely than men to welcome somewhere to write prayer requests when they visit rural churches (45% compared with 36%).

- It is the twelve to nineteen age group which is most likely to welcome somewhere to write prayer requests (52%). It is the over sixties who are least likely to welcome somewhere to write prayer requests (37%).

- While visitors in their twenties and thirties have consistently shown the lowest level of interest among the age groups in areas like wanting to find someone to welcome them, news of church services, news of church events, guide books and guide sheets, this age group is more interested than the older age groups in finding somewhere to write prayer requests.

- Visitors who live within a ten mile radius of the church are more likely than those who live at greater distances away to want to find somewhere to write prayer requests.

- Weekly churchgoers are more likely than people who attend church less often to want to find somewhere to write prayer requests.

Activities

Brainstorm your experiences of visiting churches where the opportunity is given to write prayer requests. Consider three issues. Where in the church is this opportunity given? What kind of materials (notice boards, postcards, etc.) are provided for writing prayer requests? What is proclaimed about the purpose of doing this (are the requests prayed by the clergy, etc.)?

Talking points

- Is it surprising that two out of every five visitors to rural churches would like to find somewhere to write prayer requests?

- Why are women more interested than men in finding somewhere to write prayer requests?

- How do you account for the high level of interest in finding somewhere to write prayer requests shown by twelve to nineteen year olds?

- How do you account for the level of interest shown by twenty to thirty-nine year olds in finding somewhere to write prayer requests, when this age group tends otherwise to show the lowest level of interest in other religious aspects of the churches they visit?

- What do you learn from the fact that those who live within a ten mile radius of the church are the most likely to want to find somewhere to write prayer requests?

- Why are weekly churchgoers so interested in finding somewhere to write prayer requests?

Reflection

Those churches which provide somewhere to write prayer requests seem to be fulfilling a real need among visitors. Four points are worth taking into consideration when offering such a facility.

First, visitors may prefer somewhere quiet, private and comfortable to compose their prayer requests. A side chapel set apart for quiet and for prayer can be ideal.

Second, visitors may find it helpful to place their prayer requests in a particularly sacred location. Depending on church tradition this could be near an icon, a statue, a crucifix or a place for votive candles.

Third, some churches make it known that the clergy or laity pray these prayer requests at a specific time, say at the daily offices or at the mid-week morning eucharist.

Fourth, like so many features of rural churches, someone has to be responsible for keeping a daily check on the prayer requests. Obscenities written by children, for example, can so quickly bring the whole enterprise into disrepute. Prayer requests which are left to grow yellow with age proclaim a lack of concern and of relevance to the living church community.

I thought Terry Waite had been released?

9 Flowers

Overall 66%

Sex

male	57%
female	72%

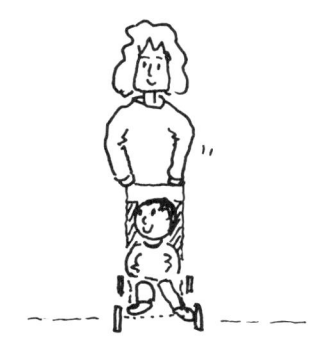

Age

12-19	74%
20-39	61%
40-59	62%
60 and over	71%

Distance travelled

under 10 miles	70%
10 miles plus	67%
outside UK	58%

Church attendance

weekly	64%
monthly	73%
less often	65%

Listening to the statistics

- Finding flowers in the church is important to two in every three (66%) of the people who visit rural churches. It is not so important to the other one in every three (34%).

- Women who visit rural churches are much more likely than men to want to find flowers in the church (72% compared with 57%).

- The two age groups who are most likely to want to find flowers in the church are the youngest and the eldest groups. Thus 74% of the 12-19 year olds and 71% of those aged 60 and over wish to find flowers, compared with 61% or 62% of those aged between 20 and 59 years.

- Visitors who have come from outside the UK are less likely to appreciate finding flowers in rural churches than is the case among visitors who live within the UK.

- Finding flowers in rural churches appeals more to those people who attend church services monthly (73%) than to those who attend weekly (64%) or who attend less than once a month (65%).

58 Rural Visitors

Activity

Invite the people who take responsibility for ensuring that there are flowers in the church to listen to how important their work is to the many people who visit rural churches. Explore whether more attention can be given to displaying flowers for the benefit of visitors rather than mainly for the benefit of regular services and for those who worship on Sundays.

Talking points

- Why should as many as 66% of the visitors to rural churches wish to find flowers in the church?

- Is it surprising that as many as 57% of the men who visit rural churches wish to find flowers there?

- How do you explain the higher level of interest in finding flowers in rural churches among both the youngest age groups (12-19 year olds) and the eldest age groups (those aged 60 and over)?

- How do you explain the fact that visitors from within the UK show a higher level of appreciation for finding flowers in rural churches than is the case among visitors who have travelled from overseas?

- What do you learn from the fact that monthly churchgoers show a greater interest in finding flowers in rural churches than is the case among those who attend church either more often or less often than monthly?

Reflection

The survey data demonstrate that finding flowers in rural churches may be much more important to church visitors than many of those responsible for flower arranging may have thought. In this sense the flower arrangers have an important ministry to church tourists. Two points may be worth keeping in mind when developing this ministry.

```
THE PARISH OF WARBLEBRIGHT

    Chief Flower Arranger........ Mrs Slowbud
    Deputy Flower Arranger...... Mrs Nosejoint
    Flower Rota Organiser......... Mrs Pottlejar-Jones
    Deputy Rota Organiser........ Miss Nettle
    Bucket Filler.................... Miss Parsnip
    Vicar.............................. The Rev'd Roger Nebnod
    Church Wardens............... Mrs Nicely & Mr Roughshod
```

First, flower arrangements can enhance the aesthetic experience of church visitors in two ways. Flowers appeal to the sense of sight with richness of colour, shape, and design. Flowers also appeal to the sense of smell with their rich and varied fragrance. Careful choice regarding where flowers are displayed can enhance both of these characteristics. For example, flowers placed in a confined space can enrich that space more fully with their aroma.

Second, flowers can stimulate profound reflection on the created order and open the door to religious experience and to theological insight. Visitors may be challenged to reflect more deeply about the religious significance of the flowers they see in rural churches by the display of a single biblical text like:

> Jesus said, 'Consider the flowers of the field; how they grow; they neither toil nor spin, yet I tell you, even Solomon in all his glory was not clothed like one of these' (Matthew 6:29).

10 Music Playing

Overall 41%

Sex

male	38%
female	43%

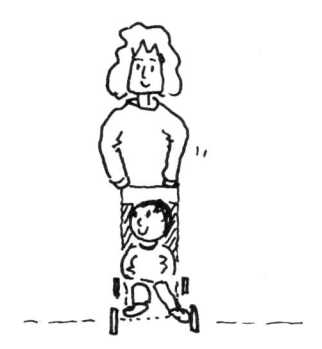

Age

12-19	55%
20-39	38%
40-59	35%
60 and over	38%

Distance travelled

under 10 miles	46%
10 miles plus	39%
outside UK	48%

Church attendance

weekly	39%
monthly	43%
less often	41%

Listening to the statistics

- Two out of every five (41%) of the visitors to rural churches welcome the ideal of finding music playing. This is not so important to the other three in every five visitors (59%).

- Finding music playing in rural churches is slightly more important to women visitors (43%) than to men visitors (38%).

- Finding music playing in rural churches is much more important to the 12-19 year old visitors (55%) than to visitors aged 20 and over.

- There is a significant link between the distance travelled to visit rural churches and the importance given to finding music playing in the church. Visitors who live under ten miles from the church (46%) and visitors from outside the UK (48%) are more likely to appreciate music playing in the church than is the case among visitors who have travelled over ten miles within the UK (39%).

- There is no clear link between the visitors' own pattern of church attendance and their views on finding music playing in the church.

Activity

Set up a simple sound system in the church and try out different kinds of music. Include, for example, reflective organ music, Gregorian chant, modern religious songs. Discuss the ways in which different types of music transform the atmosphere in the church. Which kind of music may be most helpful to church visitors?

Talking points

- Why should as many as 41% of visitors to rural churches be interested in finding music playing in the church?

- Why is a slightly higher proportion of women than men interested in finding music playing in the church?

- Why is music playing in the church likely to be more important to teenage visitors than to visitors in the older age groups?

- How do you explain the higher level of interest in music playing in the church among visitors who live under ten miles from the church than among those who live further away in the United Kingdom?

- Is it surprising that there is no clear relationship between the visitors' own pattern of church attendance and their attitude toward finding music playing in rural churches?

Reflection

Providing a sound system and music playing in rural churches may be a good idea for two reasons. To begin with, music makes an important contribution to atmosphere and may enhance the visitors' overall aesthetic experience. A number of secular tourist attractions have discovered this insight. Additionally, however, there is a long and well established link between music and religious experience. Rural churches may be able to speak more powerfully to visitors through the judicious use of music.

When providing music in rural churches three words of caution are worth keeping in mind. A poor quality sound system or one which is extended beyond its capabilities can make the more musical among the visitors feel uncomfortable. The wrong choice of music can encourage visitors to rush away rather than to linger and to reflect. While it is helpful for sound systems to be activated by opening doors or by other sensor devices, the sudden start of loud music can frighten some visitors.

In answer to the complaint that nobody could hear Tracy, Adam, James and Samantha's voices, we have invested in some amplification…..

Music can either be designed to fill the whole church or concentrated in a specific area. If a chapel is screened off (say to provide a warm area in winter) it can be effective to have music triggered by opening the door into this chapel.

11 Smell of incense

Overall 24%

Sex

male	22%
female	25%

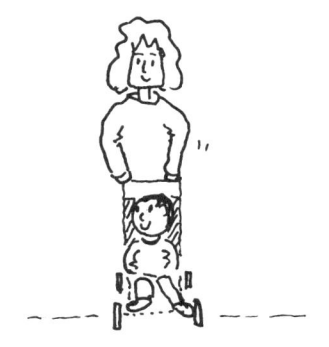

Age

12-19	47%
20-39	24%
40-59	16%
60 and over	14%

Distance travelled

under 10 miles	32%
10 miles plus	22%
outside UK –	26%

Church attendance

weekly	22%
monthly	25%
less often	25%

Listening to the statistics

- Finding the smell of incense in rural churches is important to one in every four (24%) of the visitors. It is not so important for the other three in every four (76%).

- Women and men who visit rural churches show a similar level of interest in finding the smell of incense there.

- The smell of incense in rural churches is much more important to the young visitors than to older visitors. Thus, 47% of the 12-19 year old visitors say that the smell of incense is important to them, compared with 14% of the visitors aged 60 and over.

- Finding the smell of incense in rural churches is more important to visitors who have travelled less than ten miles (32%), than to visitors who have travelled greater distances within the United Kingdom (22%), or from overseas (26%).

- The appeal of the smell of incense to those who visit rural churches is unrelated to the visitors' own pattern of church attendance. Incense is important to 22% of those who attend church weekly and to 25% of those who attend church less than weekly.

Activity

Explore different ways of introducing incense-like fragrances to your church. A particularly effective and safe method may be to warm aromatic oil on a low wattage light bulb. Discover whereabouts in the church this is most effective. Discuss how the smell changes the atmosphere in the church.

Talking points

- Why should incense be less attractive than music or flowers to visitors to rural churches?

- How significant do you feel it is that 22% of men and 25% of women who visit rural churches feel that the smell of incense is important to them?

- Why are teenage church visitors so much more interested than older church visitors in finding the smell of incense in the churches they visit?

- How do you explain the higher level of interest in the smell of incense among visitors who live under ten miles from the church they are visiting?

- Is it surprising that there is no clear relationship between the visitors' own pattern of church attendance and their attitude toward finding the smell of incense in rural churches?

Reflection

The sense of smell may sometimes speak quite loudly to those who visit rural churches. For some rural churches the dominant smell is one of dampness, fusty linen and slowly rotting hymn books. The smell of damp churches is evocative of neglect and decay. The appropriate use of incense-like fragrances can help to mask such unhelpful smells.

'INCENSE 2001'....(patents pending)

The use of incense, however, goes well beyond masking unhelpful smells. Incense-like fragrances can also help to generate an atmosphere of holiness, of peace, and of tranquillity. This is something which young people especially are rediscovering.

Churches which introduce incense-like fragrances may also wish to draw visitors' attention to ways in which the religious tradition has seen incense as a symbol for prayer or as a reminder of the presence of God. For example, Psalm 141:2 begins:

> I call upon you, O Lord; come quickly to me;
> give ear to my voice when I call to you.
> Let my prayer be counted as incense before you.

12 Candles to light

Overall 43%

Sex

| male | 36% |
| female | 46% |

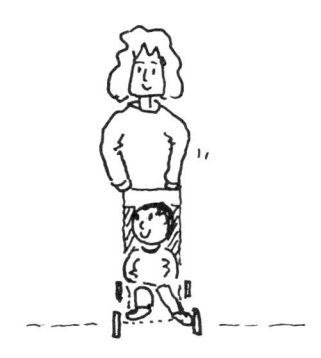

Age

12-19	67%
20-39	47%
40-59	35%
60 and over	28%

Distance travelled

under 10 miles	51%
10 miles plus	41%
outside UK	44%

Church attendance

weekly	39%
monthly	49%
less often	44%

Listening to the statistics

- Finding candles to light is important to slightly more than two in every five (43%) of the people who visit rural churches. It is not so important to the other three in every five visitors (57%).

- Women who visit rural churches are more likely than men to want to find candles to light (46% compared with 36%).

- There is a strong correlation between age and interest in finding candles to light in rural churches. While 28% of visitors aged 60 and over show an interest in lighting candles, the proportions rise to 35% among the 40-59 year olds, to 47% among the 20-39 year olds, and to 67% among the 12-19 year olds.

- Visitors who live within a ten mile radius of the church they are visiting are more likely to express an interest in finding candles to light than visitors who have travelled from further afield.

- There is an interesting relationship between the visitors' own pattern of church attendance and their interest in finding candles to light. Those most interested in lighting candles are people who attend church monthly but who are not weekly churchgoers.

Activity

If your church does not already make provision for votive candles, experiment with ways of doing this. Candles can be lighted in specially made candle holders or in a sand tray. Invite a group to come into church, to light candles and to explore the symbolism of lighting candles in church.

Talking points

- Why should as many as 43% of the visitors to rural churches be interested in finding candles to light?

- Why are women more likely than men to want to find candles to light when they visit rural churches?

- Why are younger people much more interested than older people in finding candles to light whey they visit rural churches?

- How do you explain the higher level of interest in finding candles to light among those who live within a ten mile radius of the church they are visiting?

- Why are those who attend church once a month more likely than those who attend church every week to express an interest in finding a candle to light?

Reflection

Candles continue to play an important part in the life of the church. Many churches place candles on the altar and light these throughout the service. Many churches light the Pascal candle at Easter and keep this candle burning at services throughout the Easter season. The tradition of Advent candles seems to have grown in popularity in recent years. Many churches light a candle at baptism for the newly baptised. Clearly candles can function as an important religious symbol.

The use of votive candles have become associated largely with Catholic or high church practice. This may be unfortunate if it deprives large parts of the church of access to such powerful symbolism. Lighting a votive candle may help some visitors to rural churches to focus their thoughts and to pray.

Rural churches which decide to provide votive candles may also wish to provide a very brief leaflet or card explaining the practice and the theology behind it.

There are also risks associated with providing candles that need to be taken seriously. The church insurers may need to be notified. A fire extinguisher should be placed near-by. Some churches may decide only to make votive candles available when there is a warden on duty in the church.

13 Suggestions for prayer

Overall 30%

Sex

male	27%
female	31%

Age

12-19	38%
20-39	27%
40-59	26%
60 and over	27%

Distance travelled

under 10 miles	37%
10 miles plus	29%
outside UK	23%

Church attendance

weekly	36%
monthly	32%
less often	21%

Listening to the statistics

- Nearly one in every three people who visit rural churches (30%) would welcome suggestions for prayer. This is not so important for the other two in every three visitors (70%).

- Men are almost as likely as women to welcome suggestions for prayer when they visit rural churches (27% compared with 31%).

- Teenage visitors to rural churches are more likely than older visitors to welcome suggestions for prayer (38% compared with 27%).

- Those who live less than ten miles from the church they are visiting are more likely than those who have travelled greater distances to look for suggestions for prayer.

- There is a very clear link between the visitors' own pattern of church attendance and their interest in finding suggestions for prayer. While 36% of those who attend church services weekly are interested in finding suggestions for prayer, the proportion falls to 21% among those who attend church services less than once a month.

Activity

Invite members of the group to select and bring resources which they feel may be helpful for church visitors who are seeking suggestions for prayer. Prayer cards which contain one focused and well presented prayer may be particularly helpful. Encourage the group to discuss the different suggestions.

Talking points

- Is it surprising that one in every three visitors to rural churches would welcome finding suggestions for prayer?

- Would the same kind of suggestions for prayer be likely to appeal equally to men and to women?

- How do you interpret the fact that teenage church visitors are more likely than older visitors to welcome suggestions for prayer?

- Why are those who live within ten miles of the church they are visiting more likely than those who have travelled greater distances to welcome suggestions for prayer?

- How might weekly churchgoers and occasional churchgoers differ in respect of the kind of suggestions for prayer which they would welcome when visiting rural churches?

Reflection

Often churches are called houses of prayer. The very architecture and the atmosphere of many rural churches may call visitors to remember the invitation to prayer. The fact that many church visitors are on holiday and away from their normal routine of life may also make them particularly susceptible to hearing the invitation to prayer as they find time to reflect on the meaning and purpose of their lives.

In this context it is important to remember how inadequately prepared many people now are to respond to the invitation to pray. Fewer minds are now well stocked with the prayers learnt in childhood or recited in the worship of the church. Even many people who attend church services every Sunday may suddenly discover that they have never really been taught to pray.

Rural churches which attract visitors and tourists are ideally placed to respond to a thirst for prayer by providing appropriate resources as suggestions for prayer. These resources may include free prayer cards which visitors are encouraged to take away and to continue to use. They may also include appropriate books for sale on the book stall.

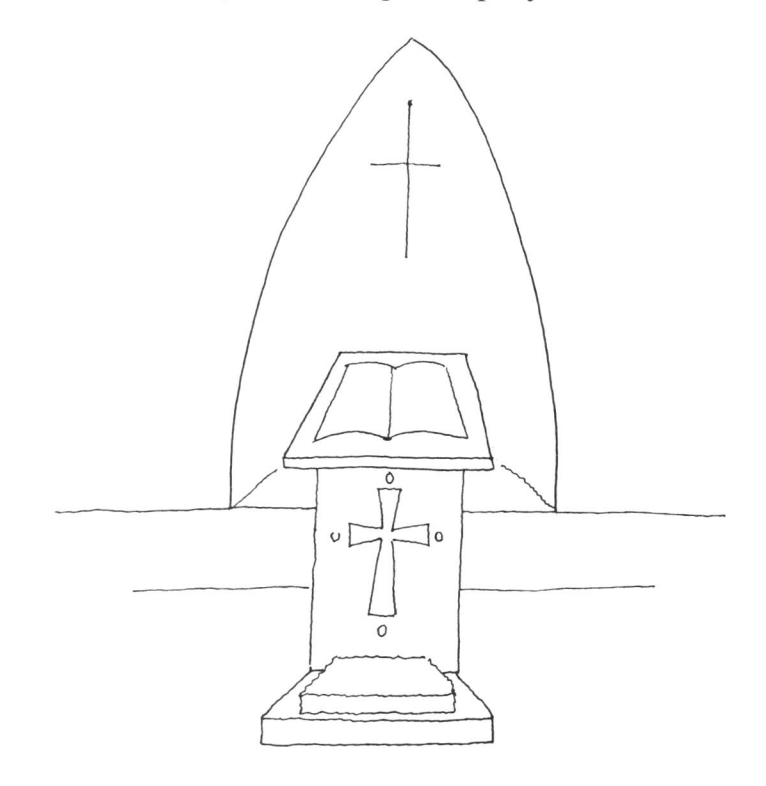

14 An open bible

Overall   46%

Sex

male	43%
female	48%

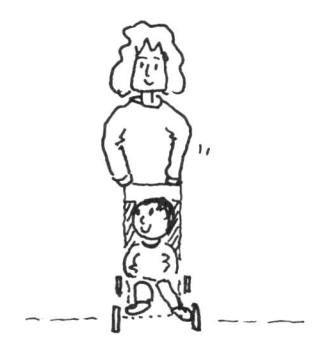

Age

12-19	52%
20-39	44%
40-59	42%
60 and over	45%

Distance travelled

under 10 miles	51%
10 miles plus	46%
outside UK	37%

Church attendance

weekly	54%
monthly	48%
less often	36%

Listening to the statistics

- Finding an open bible in the church is important to nearly half (46%) of the people who visit rural churches. It is not so important to the other 54%.

- Women who visit rural churches are slightly more likely than men to want to find an open bible in the church (48% compared with 43%).

- It is the youngest group of visitors (the 12-19 year olds) who are the most likely to want to find an open bible in the church. Thus 52% of the 12-19 year olds want to find an open bible in church, compared with 42% of those in the 40-59 year age group.

- Those who live less than ten miles from the church are more likely to want to find an open bible in the church than those who have travelled greater distances.

- There is a very clear link between the visitors' own pattern of church attendance and their views on finding an open bible in the church. While 54% of those who attend church services weekly like to find an open bible in the churches they visit, the proportion falls to 36% among those who attend church services less than once a month.

Rural Visitors

Activity

Look at the supply of bibles in your church and assess what these bibles say about the importance of the bible to the people who worship here. Are visitors attracted to look at the bible on the lectern and what would they discover if they did so?

Talking points

- Why should nearly half the visitors to rural churches be attracted to finding an open bible in the church?

- Why is a slightly higher proportion of women than men attracted to finding an open bible in the church?

- How do you account for the higher level of interest in finding an open bible in the church among the 12-19 year age group?

- How do you explain the higher level of interest in finding an open bible in the church among those who live within a ten mile radius of the church they are visiting?

- What do you make of the fact that as many as one in every three of those who do not attend church services regularly themselves are nonetheless interested in finding an open bible in the church?

Reflection

Visiting churches may present people with opportunities which they do not have in other contexts to come face to face with the bible and to read passages of scripture. While it is true that many homes possess a copy of the bible, it is equally true that many of these copies remain unopened and unread. Three points are worth considering regarding the display of open bibles in churches.

First, it is important to choose the translation carefully. The authorised version of the bible may well convey dignity and historical perspective. To people unfamiliar with modern church life, this traditional translation may also convey a note of old fashioned irrelevance.

Second, there is good sense in keeping open on the lectern the Gospel reading from the previous Sunday. A carefully printed notice can draw attention to why the passage was read on Sunday and to what it means.

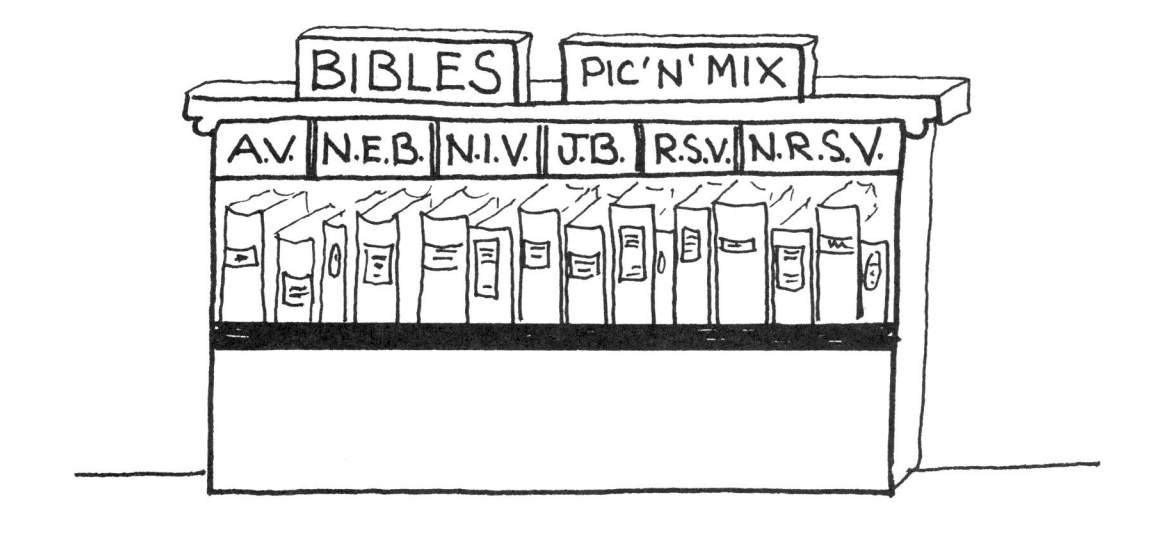

Third, there may be other places in the church, in addition to the lectern, where an open bible could attract the attention of visitors. For example, a passage on baptism could be opened near the font, and a passage on eucharist could be opened near the altar. On each occasion a brief note could draw attention to the significance of the open passage.

15 Reserved sacrament

Overall 24%

Sex

male	24%
female	24%

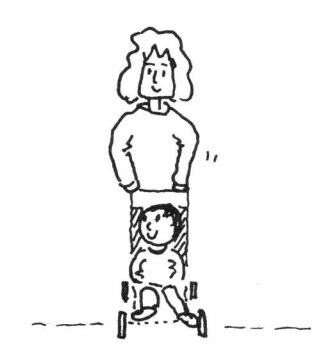

Age

12-19	34%
20-39	20%
40-59	20%
60 and over	22%

Distance travelled

under 10 miles	27%
10 miles plus	24%
outside UK	22%

Church attendance

weekly	30%
monthly	26%
less often	17%

Listening to the statistics

- Finding the reserved sacrament in church is important to one in four (24%) of the people who visit rural churches. It is not so important to the other three in every four (76%).

- Finding the reserved sacrament in church is important to the same proportions of men and women who visit rural churches.

- Finding the reserved sacrament in church is more important to the 12-19 year olds than to the other age groups. Thus, 34% of the 12-19 year olds consider it important to find the reserved sacrament in church, compared with between 20% and 22% of the older age groups.

- Finding the reserved sacrament in church is more important to those who live within a ten mile radius than those who have travelled greater distances.

- There is a clear link between the visitors' own pattern of church attendance and their views on finding the reserved sacrament in the church. While 30% of those who attend church services weekly like to find the reserved sacrament in the churches they are visiting, the proportion falls to 17% among those who attend church services less than once a month.

Activity

Making provision for the reserved sacrament in church used to be a clear statement of identifying with the Catholic wing of the Anglican church. Other practical considerations, like the availability of the sacrament for house communions among those unable to get to church and Sunday communion by extension in the absence of a priest have broadened the old churchmanship debate. Find out where the people in your church stand on this issue.

Talking points

- Why should one in four of the visitors to rural churches be interested in finding the reserved sacrament in the church?

- Why are as many men as women interested in finding the reserved sacrament in church?

- Why are the 12-19 year olds more likely to be interested in finding the reserved sacrament in church, compared with older people?

- Why are those who live within a ten mile radius of the church likely to be more interested in finding the reserved sacrament in the church than those who have travelled greater distances?

- Why is interest in finding the reserved sacrament in church so clearly correlated with the visitors' own personal pattern of church attendance?

Reflection

Historically the question of keeping and displaying the reserved sacrament in Anglican churches has been a matter of acrimonious controversy. The practice was revived by the Tractarian movement and became one of the key markers of the Catholic wing of the Anglican church.

Placing theological dispute to one side, the presence of the reserved sacrament in rural churches can provide a very important focus for holiness and for proper devotion. This is best achieved by taking seriously two considerations.

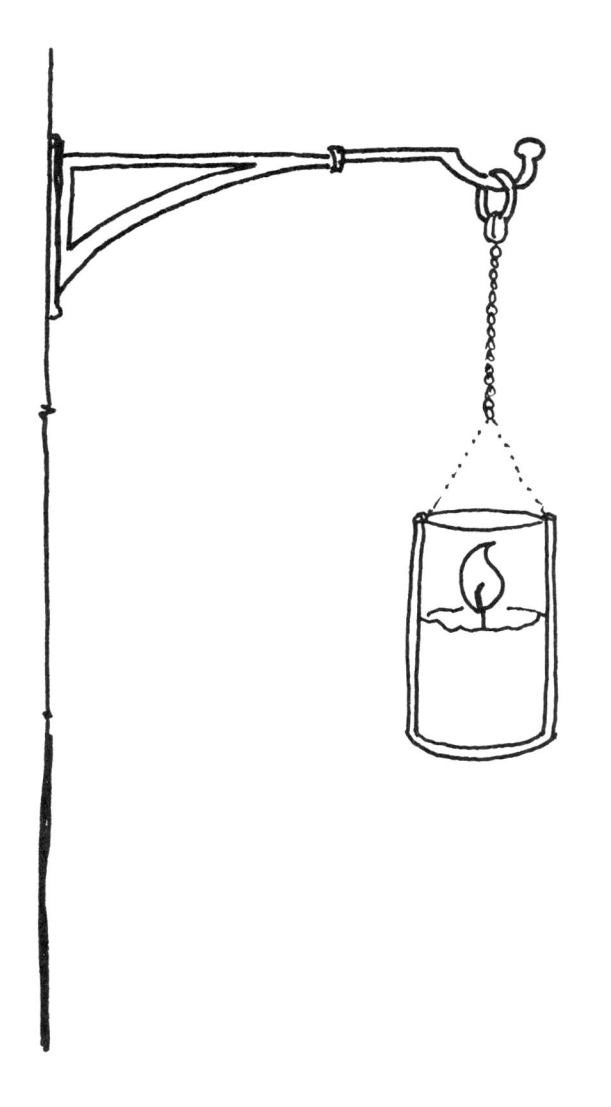

The reserved sacrament needs to be reverently located in a space where personal devotion is appropriate and private. A side chapel in which the presence of the reserved sacrament is signalled by a lamp can provide such a focus for devotion.

Some visitors will benefit from clear information explaining how in the reserved sacrament the church recognises (in one sense or another) the body and blood of Christ present in the Eucharist. It might also be helpful to provide a leaflet offering suggestions for devotions in a chapel in which the reserved sacrament is present.

16 Somewhere quiet to pray

Overall 69%

Sex

male	65%
female	72%

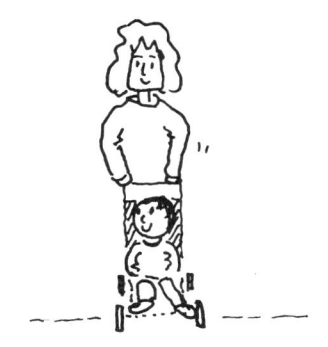

Age

12-19	65%
20-39	69%
40-59	70%
60 and over	70%

Distance travelled

under 10 miles	74%
10 miles plus	70%
outside UK	58%

Church attendance

weekly	80%
monthly	75%
less often	55%

Listening to the statistics

- A high proportion (69%) of visitors to rural churches are interested in finding somewhere quiet to pray. Fewer than one in three (31%) are not interested in this.

- Women who visit rural churches are more likely than men to want to find somewhere quiet to pray (72% compared with 65%).

- Young people between the ages of 12-19 are slightly less likely to want to find somewhere quiet to pray when they visit rural churches than is the case among older people. While 70% of visitors aged 60 and over want somewhere quiet to pray the proportion falls to 65% among the 12-19 year olds.

- Visitors who live less than ten miles from the church they are visiting are more likely to want to find somewhere quiet to pray than is the case among those who have travelled greater distances.

- Over half of the visitors who are not in the habit of attending Sunday church services at least once a month (55%) are interested in finding somewhere quiet to pray when they visit rural churches.

Activity

Spend time in the church identifying those parts of the building where it feels most comfortable to find space and quiet for personal prayer. How can these parts of the building be made even more inviting areas for quiet prayer?

Talking points

- Is it surprising that so many (69%) visitors to rural churches welcome somewhere quiet to pray?

- Is it surprising that two out of every three men (65%) who visit rural churches say that they welcome somewhere quiet to pray?

- Why does age appear to have so little effect on the proportions of visitors to rural churches who welcome somewhere quiet to pray?

- Why should visitors from outside the United Kingdom be less likely than visitors from within the United Kingdom to want to find somewhere quiet to pray?

- Over half the visitors who do not attend church services regularly themselves still want to find somewhere quiet to pray when they visit rural churches. How important do you rate this ministry extended by rural churches to visitors?

Reflection

One of the key characteristics of life today concerns the way in which so many people fill their lives with sound. The radio or television may be switched on first thing in the morning and stay switched on throughout the day.

For some people, therefore, an old country church may provide an oasis of quiet within a world which is otherwise saturated with sound. Sometimes the very architecture of the country church encourages a hushed atmosphere which in turn encourages visitors to remain quiet or to speak with one another in subdued tones.

Special environments and special atmospheres of this nature may stimulate in some people a yearning for God and a desire to pray. It is all too easy, however, for churches to destroy such fleeting opportunities. People who are unaccustomed to praying may need to be helped to find an unobtrusive spot in which they can be quiet and pray in private.

It is important, too, that positive ideas to introduce music, commentary and wardens to rural churches should not destroy the opportunities to find somewhere quiet to pray which are clearly valued by so many visitors to rural churches.

17 Christian book stall

Overall   42%

Sex

male	37%
female	45%

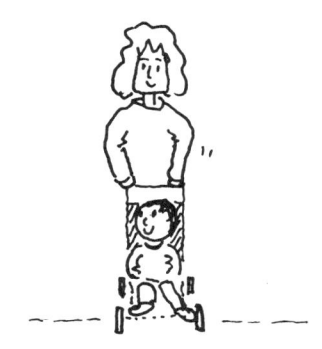

Age

12-19	45%
20-39	34%
40-59	40%
60 and over	46%

Distance travelled

under 10 miles	44%
10 miles plus	43%
outside UK	29%

Church attendance

weekly	56%
monthly	43%
less often	26%

Listening to the statistics

- Two out of every five (42%) visitors to rural churches are interested in finding a Christian book stall. This is not so important to the other three in every five visitors (58%).

- Women who visit rural churches are more likely than men to want to find a Christian book stall (45% compared with 37%).

- Christian book stalls in rural churches market more successfully to some age groups than to others. Christian book stalls are of greater interest to 12-19 year olds (45%) and to those aged sixty and over (46%) than to 20-39 year olds (34%) or to 40-59 year olds (40%).

- Christian book stalls are of greater interest to visitors who live within the United Kingdom (between 43% and 44%) than to visitors from overseas (29%).

- There is a very clear link between the visitors' own pattern of church attendance and their interest in finding a Christian book stall in the churches they visit. While 56% of those who attend church services regularly are interested in finding a Christian book stall, the proportions fall to 43% among those who attend church services at least once a month and to 26% among those who attend less than once a month.

Activity

Look at the book stalls in several rural churches. Note the titles of the books on display and evaluate the attractiveness of the stock. How viable is it to maintain an attractive book stall in rural churches? What books would you like to see for sale in your church? How can you find out what kind of books visitors will purchase from your church?

Talking points

- Why are two out of every five visitors to rural churches interested in finding a Christian book stall in the church?

- Why are women more likely than men to be interested in finding a Christian book stall in the rural churches which they visit?

- What are the implications for the book trade that different age groups show different levels of interest in finding a Christian book stall in the churches they visit?

- What are the implications for the book trade that visitors from overseas show a lower level of interest in finding a Christian bookstall, in comparison with visitors from within the United Kingdom?

- If 56% of weekly churchgoers show an interest in finding a Christian book stall in rural churches, should churches be doing more to provide Christian literature among their active members?

Reflection

Currently Christian and general publishers produce more good quality books for the religious market than the religious book trade is able to sell successfully. Good books are being published which many potential purchasers fail to see. There are two ways in which rural churches could respond to this problem and at the same time respond to a perceived need among those who visit rural churches.

This is the latest book the Vicar has acquired for the 'New Book Stall. It's great reading, and is called 'St Augustine's Confessions'

First, rural churches could develop the church book stall by holding a wider range of stock, carefully selected to appeal to different segments of the market. For example, parents and grandparents may be interested in buying Christian literature for their children and grandchildren. Young adults may be interested in buying guides to prayer and to the bible. Book stalls are unlikely to make a profit and may well make a loss as stock is stolen or damaged. Provision of a book stall should be seen as part of the local church's mission both to the local community and to visitors.

Second, rural churches could develop ways of drawing attention to recent Christian books which are not on sale in the church but which could be obtained from other bookshops or by post. Publishers may well be interested in providing churches with promotional materials or display materials for appropriate titles.

18 Requests for donations

Overall 41%

Sex

male	40%
female	42%

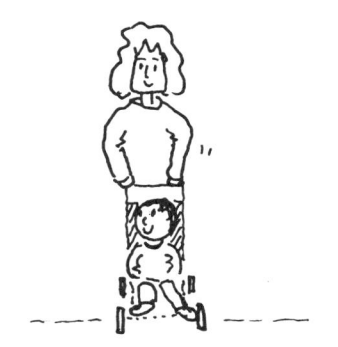

Age

12-19	52%
20-39	38%
40-59	35%
60 and over	41%

Distance travelled

under 10 miles	41%
10 miles plus	42%
outside UK	34%

Church attendance

weekly	40%
monthly	44%
less often	41%

Listening to the statistics

- Finding requests for donations is important to two in every five (41%) of the people who visit rural churches. The other three in every five (59%) are not so eager to welcome requests for donations.

- Roughly the same proportions of men and women who visit rural churches want to find requests for donations (40% and 42%).

- Young visitors between the ages of 12 and 19 are more likely than older visitors to want to find requests for donations. The largest contrast is between 52% of the 12-19 year olds and 35% of the 40-59 year olds who want to find requests for donations.

- Visitors who live in the United Kingdom are more likely to welcome requests for donations than is the case among visitors from overseas (41% or 42% compared with 34%).

- People who attend church services less than once a month are just as likely to welcome requests for donations as people who attend church services once a week (41% and 40%).

Activity

There are many different ways in which churches make requests for donations. Examine the different messages sent out by churches in your area. Then compare these with the messages sent out by your own church. What kind of message does your church really want to convey to parishioners and to visitors?

Talking points

- Is it surprising that two out of every five visitors to rural churches welcome requests for donations?

- Why are women and men equally likely to welcome requests for donations?

- Why should young people between the ages of 12 and 19 be more likely to welcome requests for donations than is the case among older visitors to rural churches?

- Why are visitors from outside the United Kingdom less likely than visitors from within the United Kingdom to welcome requests for donations?

- Why are people who attend church services infrequently as likely as weekly churchgoers to welcome requests for donations?

Reflection

There is no doubt that rural churches are expensive to maintain. A lot of time and energy is invested by rural clergy and rural congregations in raising funding for maintaining fabric. One of the very clear messages which comes from the present survey concerns the considerable extent to which this investment fulfils a ministry and mission among visitors and tourists as well as among the congregation and local residents.

The question, then, is to what extent and in which ways visitors and tourists can be asked to contribute to the upkeep of the churches they visit?

Many churches now find it very helpful to draw a firm distinction between two kinds of appeals for money. One purse properly pays for the ministry of the church. Another purse pays for the upkeep of the church building. When visitors are asked for money they have the right to know into which purse they are contributing.

A much wider pool of people may want to contribute to the upkeep of the church building than may want to support the wider work of the church. It is helpful, too, to let potential donors know about the specific upkeep costs for which their contributions will be used.

19 Access for the disabled

Overall 70%

Sex

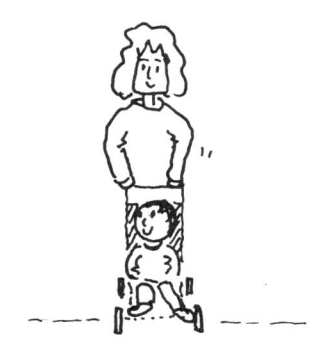

male	63%
female	75%

Age

12-19	80%
20-39	66%
40-59	66%
60 and over	70%

Distance travelled

under 10 miles	70%
10 miles plus	71%
outside UK	60%

Church attendance

weekly	72%
monthly	72%
less often	67%

Listening to the statistics

- Concern for disabled access is now widely shared within society, with 70% of visitors to rural churches considering that this is important.

- Women who visit rural churches are more concerned about access for the disabled than is the case among men who visit rural churches (75% compared with 63%).

- Young people between the ages of 12 and 19 years are more likely to be concerned about access for the disabled than is the case among older people. While 80% of the 12-19 year olds feel that it is important to find access for the disabled, the proportion falls to 66% among the 20-59 year olds.

- Visitors who live within the United Kingdom give a higher priority to finding access for the disabled than is the case among visitors who have travelled from outside the United Kingdom (70% or 71% compared with 60%).

- People who attend church services at least once a month give a higher priority to finding access for the disabled than is the case among those who attend church services less frequently (72% compared with 67%).

Activity

Borrow a wheel chair and explore how difficult or how easy it is to visit your church in a wheel chair. Begin from where the disabled visitor is expected to park the car. Assume you do not know through which door to enter and see how well entry is signposted. Pay particular attention to the steps at the main entrance and between the nave and the chancel. How friendly is your church for disabled access?

Talking points

- Why are so many people now concerned about access for the disabled to rural churches?

- Why are women more likely to be concerned about access for the disabled than is the case among men?

- Why are young people between the ages of 12 and 19 years more likely to be concerned about access for the disabled than is the case among older people?

- Why are visitors who live within the United Kingdom more likely than visitors who live outside the United Kingdom to give priority to finding access for the disabled?

- Why are regular churchgoers more likely than less frequent churchgoers to give priority to finding access for the disabled?

Reflection

The majority of rural churches were designed and built in an age when much less attention was given to the needs of the disabled than is the case today. As a consequence many rural churches continue to find it quite difficult to effect the modifications necessary to improve access for the disabled. Nonetheless many imaginative schemes have been initiated in rural churches which are worth publicising and from which other churches can learn.

Access for the disabled is concerned with many issues in addition to wheel chair access. A careful safety audit of the rural church could bring to light many potential hazards for the partially sighted and for those with various mobility difficulties. Uneven floor surfaces and concealed steps can prove particularly hazardous to those who are unfamiliar with the building.

If access is not altogether safe it may be wise to close off certain parts of the church.

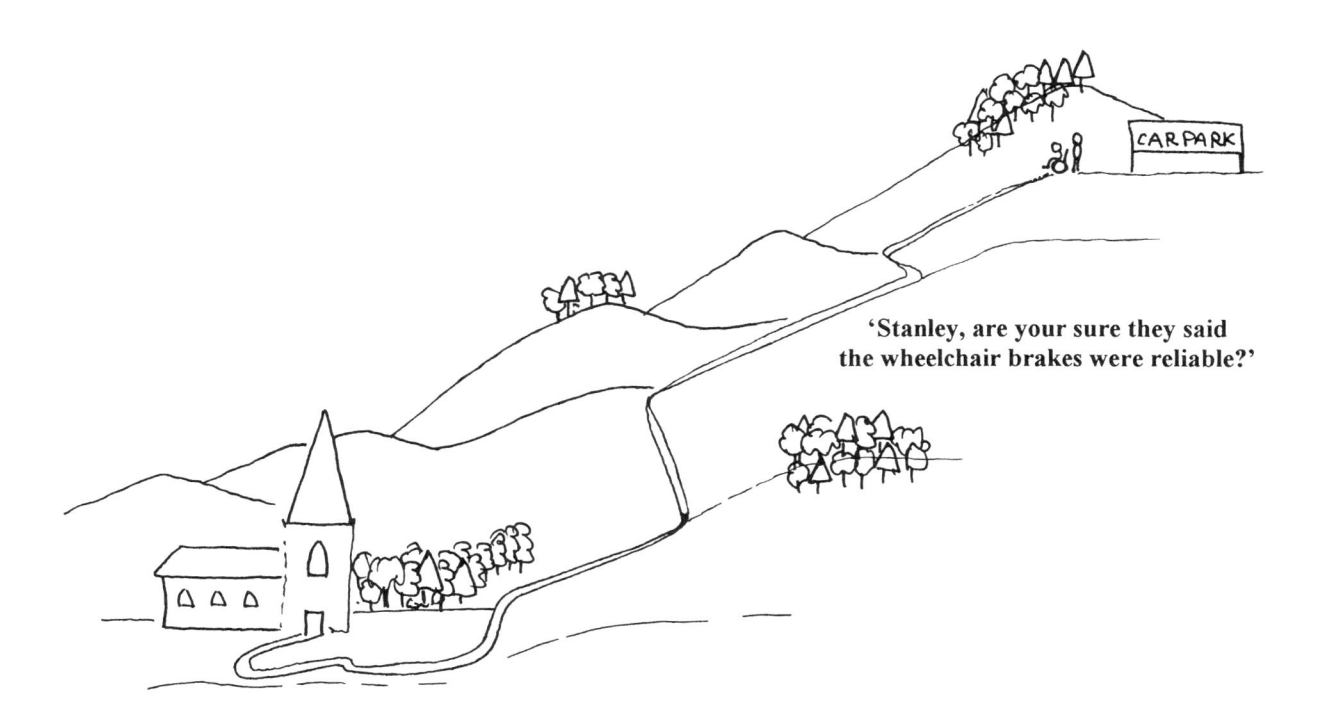

'Stanley, are your sure they said the wheelchair brakes were reliable?'

20 Gifts to buy

Overall 34%

Sex

male	30%
female	37%

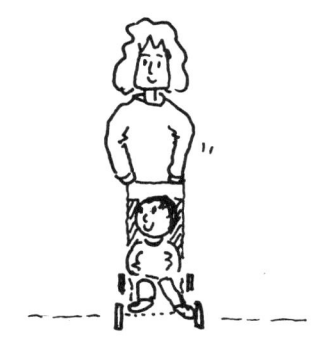

Age

12-19	58%
20-39	31%
40-59	26%
60 and over	25%

Distance travelled

under 10 miles	42%
10 miles plus	34%
outside UK	30%

Church attendance

weekly	32%
monthly	39%
less often	35%

Listening to the statistics

- Finding gifts to buy is important to one in every three visitors to rural churches (34%). It is not so important to the other two in every three visitors (66%).

- Women who visit rural churches show a higher level of interest than the men in finding gifts to buy (37% compared with 30%).

- Young people between the ages of 12 and 19 are much more interested than older people in finding gifts to buy when they visit rural churches. While 58% of 12-19 year olds indicate an interest in finding gifts to buy, the proportions fall to 31% among 20-39 year olds and to 25% among those aged 60 and over.

- The visitors who are most likely to want to find gifts to buy are those who have travelled the least distance. Thus, 42% of those who live within a ten mile radius want to find gifts to buy, compared with 34% of those who have travelled ten miles or more.

- People who attend church services weekly are less likely than other visitors to want to find gifts to buy.

Activities

Take a good look at the souvenirs on sale in shops in the area. Why do people buy such souvenirs? Are there souvenirs which could be sold in the local church? What would be the implications of selling gifts in the local church?

Talking points

- Is it surprising that one in every three visitors to rural churches would like to find gifts to buy?

- Why is a slightly higher proportion of women than men interested in finding gifts to buy when they visit rural churches?

- How do you explain the much higher level of interest in gifts to buy among the 12-19 year olds who visit rural churches?

- Why should people who live within a ten mile radius of the church they are visiting be more interested than visitors who have travelled further in finding gifts to buy?

- Why are people who attend church services weekly less interested in finding gifts to buy?

Reflection

The idea of selling gifts in churches is distasteful to some, but may be seen as providing imaginative opportunities by others.

Many visitors who are on holiday may be attracted by purchasing small and inexpensive souvenirs, including postcards, packs of greeting cards showing the church, pens, pencils and so on. Relatively inexpensive items can be left in the church on the trust that visitors will pay for them.

The Vicar decided to do a little advertising while out visiting

Churches which maintain a rota of wardens may find that a wider range of things on sale provide greater interest both for the visitors and for the wardens. The church shop can provide a useful outlet for local crafts and for local produce in season. Some churches provide a useful display area for local artists whose work can be purchased in the church. Others display in a secure cabinet items that be bought in a nearby shop on behalf of church funds. Churches which trade in this kind of way need to provide adequate security for the wardens.

21 Information about other things to do in the area

Overall 44%

Sex

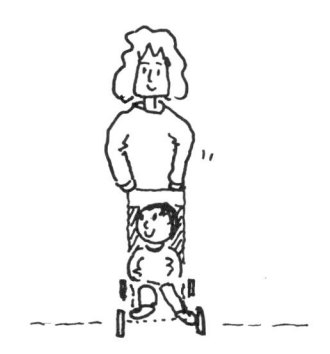

male	41%
female	46%

Age

12-19	64%
20-39	47%
40-59	36%
60 and over	36%

Distance travelled

under 10 miles	51%
10 miles plus	44%
outside UK	38%

Church attendance

weekly	38%
monthly	47%
less often	50%

Listening to the statistics

- Finding information about other things to do in the area is important to 44% of the people who visit rural churches. It is not so important to the other 56%.

- Women who visit rural churches are slightly more likely than men to want to find information about other things to do in the area (46% compared with 41%).

- Expectation regarding finding information about other things to do in the area is clearly related to age. While 64% of the 12-19 year olds feel it important to find information about other things to do in the area, the proportions fall to 47% among the 20-39 year olds and to 36% among those aged 40 and over.

- Those who live less than ten miles from the church are more likely than those who live further away to value finding information about other things to do in the area.

- There is a clear inverse relationship between the visitors' own pattern of church attendance and their interest in finding information about other things to do in the area. Thus 38% of weekly churchgoers welcome finding information about other things to do in the area, compared with 47% of those who attend church at least once a month, and 50% of those who attend church less than once a month.

Activity

Undertake a review of the things to do in the area which might appeal to the people who visit your church. Examine how well these things are advertised and promoted in the area. How can your church help to make these things known? Would it also be helpful for information about your church to be promoted by other places in the area which attract tourists?

Talking points

- Is it realistic for 44% of church visitors to expect rural churches to display information about other things to do in the area?

- Why is a slightly higher proportion of women than men interested in finding information about other things to do in the area?

- How do you explain the higher level of interest in information about other things to do in the area expressed by the 20-39 year olds, compared with 40-59 year olds?

- Why are people who live within a ten mile radius of the church likely to show a higher level of interest than those who have travelled further distances in information about other things to do in the area?

- Why are weekly churchgoers less likely to be interested in information about other things to do in the area, in comparison with those who attend church less frequently?

Reflection

Rural churches can either see themselves as standing very clearly apart from the general rural tourist industry or as working as an integral part of this industry. There are three important arguments for encouraging rural churches to work in collaboration with the wider rural tourist industry.

First, by attracting more visitors rural churches may contribute more effectively to the local economy. Local shops, guesthouses, and other tourist attractions all stand to benefit.

Second, by attracting more visitors rural churches stand to benefit financially if visitors are encouraged to make donations or to make purchases from the church shop.

Third, by developing their ministry to tourists rural churches have the opportunity to invite visitors to consider the claims of the Christian gospel, to read scripture, to pray, and to recommit themselves to Christ. In this way the old stones of the rural church are given the opportunity to proclaim their faith to a new generation and in a new way.

Churches which provide information about other tourist attractions in the area can invite those places to reciprocate by providing information about churches in the area.

22 Toilet

Overall 48%

Sex

male	43%
female	51%

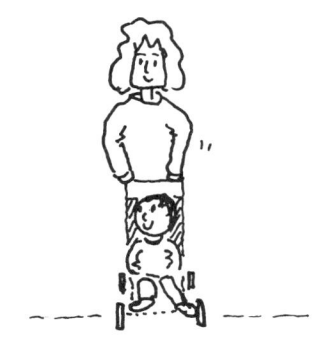

Age

12-19	67%
20-39	44%
40-59	40%
60 and over	46%

Distance travelled

under 10 miles	52%
10 miles plus	48%
outside UK	46%

Church attendance

weekly	50%
monthly	49%
less often	45%

Listening to the statistics

- Half of the visitors to rural churches (48%) would welcome finding toilets within or near the church.

- The importance of finding toilets within or near rural churches is emphasised by a higher proportion of women visitors than by men visitors (51% compared with 43%).

- Young people are much more inclined than older people to feel that it is important for rural churches to provide toilets. This view is taken by 67% of 12-19 year olds, compared with 40% of 40-59 year olds.

- Visitors who have travelled from outside the United Kingdom are less likely to feel that it is important for rural churches to provide toilets (46% compared with 52% of those who live within ten miles of the church).

- Weekly churchgoers are more likely than people who attend church less than once a month to feel that it is important for rural churches to provide toilets (50% compared with 45%).

Activity

Draw up a plan of where visitors can find toilets in the local area and note the times of day when these toilets are available for use. Include local garages, inns and tea-rooms as appropriate. Examine the policy of the local authority for providing and maintaining public conveniences. Does the local church have any responsibility or capability for meeting the needs of tourists in this way?

Talking points

- Is it reasonable for 48% of those who visit rural churches to expect toilet facilities to be provided?

- Why should young people in the 12-19 year age range be so much more likely to expect rural churches to provide toilets?

- Why are visitors from outside the United Kingdom less likely to expect rural churches to provide toilets?

- Why are weekly churchgoers more likely than occasional churchgoers to expect rural churches to provide toilets?

Reflection

The majority of rural churches were built in an age before good toilet facilities became an essential feature of public buildings. In recent years considerable interest has been shown in redeveloping rural churches in ways which increase their usefulness to the local congregation and to the wider local community. As yet less attention has been given to ways in which these churches can be developed to contribute more effectively to the rural tourist industry.

**That's our toilet.
It's only for the really desperate**

The provision of toilet facilities could be of benefit to the local congregation, to the wider local community, and to the rural tourist industry. For such facilities to be properly maintained the rural church would need to draw on resources provided by the wider community.

Appendix A

Useful books :

English Churches and Visitors, Max Hanna, English Tourist Board, 1984, ISBN 086 143 1146.

Rural Tourism and Sustainable Rural Development, Eds : Bill Bramwell & Bernard Lane, Channel View Publications, 1994, ISBN 187 315 0024.

Tourism and Recreation in Rural Areas, Eds : Richard Butler, Michael Hall & John Jenkins, John Wiley, 1998, ISBN 047 197 6806.

Economic impact of recreation and tourism in the English countryside (CRN Research Reports), Countryside Agency, 2001.

The Business of Rural Tourism : International perspectives, Stephen Page & Don Getz, International Thomson Business Press, 1997, ISBN 041 513 5117.

Open All Hours - A way forward for Church buildings in the 21st century, Susan Rowe, ACORA, 2001, ISBN 0 9516871 7 4.

Bridging the Gap - The Church in the local community, Ed : Revd Canon Jeremy Martineau, ACORA, 1999, ISBN 0 9516871 5 8.

Sustainable Rural Tourism : Opportunities for local action, Countryside Commission, 1995, ISBN 086 170 4649.

From Tourist Attractions to Heritage Tourism, Pat Yale, 2nd edition ELM Publications, 1998, ISBN 185 450 1895.

Emergency Rescue Plan - available free from Sarah Crossland, Rotherham Churches Tourism Initiative. Tel 0777 987 5642.

Appendix B

Helpful organisations :

National Churches Tourism Group, Arthur Rank Centre, National Agricultural Centre, Stoneleigh Park, Warwickshire CV8 2LZ.
www.geocities.com/nctg_uk

District Council Economic Development Departments.

Regional Tourism Boards.

Appendix C

Book shop suppliers :

Tim Tiley Prints, 157 Cheltenham Road, Bristol BS6 5RR.
Distributors of printed material and Christian gift items.

Rosiglas, 6 Laburnum Grove, Bilton, Rugby CV22 7QB.
Hand painted glass candle holders at budget prices.
www.rosiglas.co.uk

Christian Enquiry Agency, 35-41 Lower Marsh, London SE1 7RL.
Tel no. 020 7620 4444.

You Matter TO US

PLEASE CIRCLE THE NUMBER AGAINST YOUR ANSWER

How far away from here do you live?

Less than 10 miles	1
10-30 miles	2
Over 30 miles	3

Are you visiting

On your own	1
With one other person	2
With 2 or 3 others	3
With between 4 and 9 others	4
with 10-19 others	5
With more than 19 others	6

How did you travel to this church?

On foot	1
By bicycle	2
By car	3
By public transport	4

Are you

Male	1
Female	2

Do you normally live in

England	1
Ireland	2
Scotland	3
Wales	4
Elsewhere – Which Country?	5

What is your age group?

0-5	1
6-11	2
12-19	3
20-39	4
40-59	5
Over 60	6

How many other churches have you visited in the last 7 days other than for worship?

None	0
One	1
Two	2
Three	3
Four	4
Five or more	5

How much do you like to find these features when you visit a church?
How much did you find in this church?
THE HIGHER THE NUMBER THE MORE YOU LIKE IT!

	What you like to find	What you did find
Someone to welcome you	5 4 3 2 1	5 4 3 2 1
News of church services	5 4 3 2 1	5 4 3 2 1
News of church events	5 4 3 2 1	5 4 3 2 1
News of local events	5 4 3 2 1	5 4 3 2 1
A guide book to buy	5 4 3 2 1	5 4 3 2 1
Simple free guide sheet	5 4 3 2 1	5 4 3 2 1
A book to write your name in	5 4 3 2 1	5 4 3 2 1
Somewhere to write prayer requests	5 4 3 2 1	5 4 3 2 1
Flowers	5 4 3 2 1	5 4 3 2 1
Music playing	5 4 3 2 1	5 4 3 2 1
Smell of incense	5 4 3 2 1	5 4 3 2 1
Candles to light	5 4 3 2 1	5 4 3 2 1
Suggestions for prayer	5 4 3 2 1	5 4 3 2 1
An open bible	5 4 3 2 1	5 4 3 2 1
Reserved sacrament	5 4 3 2 1	5 4 3 2 1
Somewhere quiet to pray	5 4 3 2 1	5 4 3 2 1
Christian book stall	5 4 3 2 1	5 4 3 2 1
Requests for donations	5 4 3 2 1	5 4 3 2 1
Access for the disabled	5 4 3 2 1	5 4 3 2 1
Gifts to buy	5 4 3 2 1	5 4 3 2 1
Information about other things to do in the area	5 4 3 2 1	5 4 3 2 1
Toilet	5 4 3 2 1	5 4 3 2 1

How did you rate this church?

Interesting	5 4 3 2 1	Boring
Holy	5 4 3 2 1	Ordinary
Welcoming	5 4 3 2 1	Off putting
Friendly	5 4 3 2 1	Unfriendly

Do you go to church on Sundays at least

Once a week	1
Once a month	2
Once a year	3
Less often	4

TODAY'S DATE

/   1999

Time   :

If you have any further comments please add them here

Thank you for your help. please place this survey in the post box in this church